LEADERSHIP CAPACITY

for LASTING SCHOOL IMPROVEMENT

Linda Lambert

Association for Supervision and Curriculum Development
Alexandria, Virginia USA

Association for Supervision and Curriculum Development
1703 N. Beauregard St. • Alexandria, VA 22311-1714 USA
Telephone: 800-933-2723 or 703-578-9600 • Fax: 703-575-5400
Web site: http://www.ascd.org • E-mail: member@ascd.org

Gene R. Carter, *Executive Director;* Nancy Modrak, *Director of Publishing;* Julie Houtz, *Director of Book Editing & Production;* Ernesto Yermoli, *Project Manager;* Shelley Young, *Senior Graphic Designer;* Cynthia Stock, *Typesetter.*

All Web links in this book are correct as of the publication date below but may have become inactive or otherwise modified since that time. If you notice a deactivated or changed link, please e-mail books@ascd.org with the words "Link Update" in the subject line. In your message, please specify the Web link, the book title, and the page number on which the link appears.

Printed in the United States of America.

July 2003 PC member book.

ISBN: 0-87120-778-8   ASCD product no.: 102283
ASCD member price: $18.95   nonmember price: $23.95

Library of Congress Cataloging-in-Publication Data

Lambert, Linda, 1939–
    Leadership capacity for lasting school improvement / Linda Lambert.
        p. cm.
Includes bibliographical references and index.
    ISBN 0-87120-778-8 (alk. paper)
    1. Educational leadership—United States. 2. Teacher participation in administration—United States. 3. School improvement programs—United States. I. Title.

    LB2805.L28 2003
    371.2—dc21   2003007080

12 11 10 09 08 07 06 05 04 03   12 11 10 9 8 7 6 5 4 3 2 1

This book is dedicated to my grandchildren—Eric Morita and Ashley Lambert; Shannon Pintane; Jered and Jessica Johnson; Chloe and Dylan Smock; and Keely, Catherine, Madeline, and John Lambert—whose love, laughter, and joy in learning inspire and enrich my life. It is my deepest hope that this new generation of children will one day contribute to the leadership capacity of their communities.

LEADERSHIP CAPACITY *for*
LASTING SCHOOL IMPROVEMENT

Foreword

In the pages that follow, Linda Lambert builds on the success of her third book, *Building Leadership Capacity in Schools* (1998), to further help us get from where we *are* to where we *want* to be. Leadership capacity, we learn, depends on understanding the connection between participation and skillfulness. Linda helps us understand how to develop participation and create structures that let educators work and learn together and share leadership responsibilities.

Leadership is about contributing to, learning from, and influencing the learning of others. But it is also about creating the opportunities for others to learn: when skillfully approached, professional development is as much about *adult* learning as student learning. Adults learn to be colleagues when they are able to practice *being* colleagues—and in doing so, to understand that students can be colleagues as well. The impor-

tance of building reciprocal rather than dependent relationships is at the heart of Linda's conception of leadership capacity, and this book teaches us not only the differences between dependency and reciprocity, but also how to move from the former to the latter.

A major tenet of leadership capacity is that development of teacher leadership should include students as well as fellow educators. Connecting participation to skill and adult learning to student learning allows us to think effectively about leadership and to embrace a vision of a school culture that supports—rather than thwarts—teachers.

Teacher leadership does not replace, but rather augments, principal leadership. Throughout this book, Linda shows us the varied means that principals use to control or open up participation, and how they can move along a continuum of enhanced learning and greater capacity.

In her chapter on teachers as leaders, Linda uses real-life examples from school districts to show how teachers grow into leadership roles, providing an inside look at the many different forms that leadership takes and the different paths that can be taken to achieve it. Activities, benchmarks, and rubrics throughout the book help us understand the processes and practices necessary for building this view of leadership. In guiding us through the subject, Linda proves a sensitive and clearly experienced guide.

Teaching and learning involve all of us in leadership. In this book, Linda helps us learn about our roles as district leaders, teachers, principals, parents, and students. Few authors have ever attempted to conceptualize the practices of leaders who are willing to make their leadership struggles public. Linda has done precisely that, inviting the reader to perceive leadership as the process of releasing the energy, intelligence, and participation of the entire school community. Viewing leadership as primarily in the service of developing a healthy organization, we learn that learning and leading are intricately tied—and that we can all become leaders as well as teachers.

—Ann Lieberman

Preface

The concept of leadership capacity has captured the imagination of educators around the world. Professionals from as far away as Tasmania, Zimbabwe, Germany, and England have responded to the central idea of my 1998 book *Building Leadership Capacity in Schools*: that sustainable development in schools is enhanced when we engage principals, teachers, parents, and students in broad-based, skillful participation in the work of leadership.

In the pursuit of high-stakes accountability, professional development has too often focused on student learning at the expense of teachers. Heresy, you say? Student-focused professional development is certainly necessary, but we need to pay attention to adult concerns as well. In airplanes we are told that in the case of an emergency, we should put on our own oxygen masks before helping children with theirs, because adults can't help children unless they are breathing properly themselves. The same principle applies to schools. We need to create an environment of discretion, autonomy, reciprocity, and professionalism before we can effectively teach those characteristics to students. And we need to join with other adults—parents and community members alike—in order to create a life of learning for all children.

Since the publication of *Building Leadership Capacity in Schools*, I have had the opportunity to work with thousands of principals, teachers, and district professionals. I have been uniformly impressed by the courage and commitment to school improvement exhibited by the educators with whom I spoke. The substance and uniformity of their comments sparked my interest in a second book on leadership capacity. I listened as the same kinds of questions surfaced repeatedly in country after country, and was puzzled by the consistency of concerns. How could such disparate educational systems give rise to the exact same issues? Yet I heard the following questions and statements over and over again:

- How will the concept of leadership capacity change my role as principal? My teachers want *me* to make the decisions. Do I now have to give up my authority and responsibilities?
- What do I do about the resistant, hard-to-change teacher?
- Some teachers just don't want to be leaders.
- How will we find the time to build leadership capacity, especially at a time when all that seem to matter are standardized test scores?
- How can we become skillful enough to build leadership capacity appropriately? Our professional development has focused on classroom skills, not adult-to-adult ones.
- How do we build sustainable commitment among professionals?
- How do we replace principals without starting all over again?
- Parents as leaders? I can hardly satisfy them *now*; I don't need them even more empowered!
- I understand the concept of "leadership capacity," but how do I achieve it?

These questions and comments form the basis for this book.

Most educators are concerned with their legacies: they don't want to look over their shoulders at a school they left three years ago to find that the improvements they'd helped introduce have been reversed or neglected. Luckily, it is possible to develop the leadership capacity of schools and districts so that improvements remain, adults keep learning, and student performance continues to advance. Leadership capacity offers us the promise of sustainable school improvement by

- Developing formal leaders as thoughtful, focused, and collaborative instructional leaders;
- Turning all adults within the school community—teachers, staff, parents, and community members—into reflective, skillful coleaders;
- Achieving steady and lasting improvement in student performance and development; and
- Constructing schools and districts that are sustainable learning organizations.

Our guide in this book is Jennifer Fielding, a teacher who transferred to Belvedere Middle School four years ago. The principal had left Belvedere the summer she arrived, prompting the school to revert back to the condition it had been in prior to his tenure. In Chapter 1, we catch up with Jennifer four years into her job at the school, as she contemplates applying for the principalship. Jennifer's example will prove useful as we examine the changing roles of teachers, principals, students, parents, and district personnel. Each chapter of this book is accompanied by guidelines, tools, questions, and activities; the appendixes include additional activities, a rubric, a continuum, surveys, and policies. *Leadership Capacity for Lasting School Improvement* is more extensive than my previous book on the subject, and will enable educators to more fully implement the concept of "leadership capacity" in schools and districts.

—Linda Lambert

Acknowledgments

First, I wish to thank the remarkable educators in Alberta and Manitoba, Canada; Kansas City, Kansas; Scottsbluff, Nebraska; Columbus, Ohio; Carlisle, Pennsylvania; Wauwatosa, Wisconsin; Richmond, San Leandro, Cupertino, Hayward, Oakland, Hickman, and Saratoga, California; and Melbourne, Australia. The educators in these districts, towns, and schools provided the examples and stories that bring this book to life. Their commitment and energy represent our best hope for educating all students well.

I have met some new colleagues during the course of my research—individuals whose questions and writings have helped to frame the issues of leadership capacity. In this regard, I wish to thank Gus Jacobs, Rosemary Foster, Greg Netzer, Ann Conzemius, Jan O'Neil, Bill Bragg, Marty Krovetz, and my longtime colleague and friend, Mary Gardner.

I am especially touched that Ann Lieberman agreed to write the foreword for this book. Her work in collaboration, teacher leadership, and networking has been a constant inspiration throughout the years. Thank you, Ann.

Finally, I want to thank my two editors. My veteran editor Morgan Lambert—also my friend, colleague, mentor, and husband—challenges me with tender wisdom to think deeply about what I observe and the conclusions that I draw. My new editor, Anne Meek of ASCD, has been a sparkling, supportive, and incisive guide in the development of this book.

CHAPTER 1
Deepening the Concept

In 1998, teacher Jennifer Fielding was attracted by the energy and innovations at Belvedere Middle School, across town from where she worked. That fall she asked for and received an in-district transfer to the school. As soon as she arrived, however, she was disappointed: the principal had left, preliminary reforms had failed to materialize, and naysayers had gained new prominence. It looked as though the school would soon revert to its old ways.

The new principal, John Trevor, and a few strong teacher leaders responded wisely. After careful thought and assessment, Principal Trevor saw that his challenge was to reaffirm and build on the reforms that had begun, break through the barriers inhibiting further progress and change, and assure staff that he would remain until plans were well implemented. Rather than reclaim the authority that had been shared, he

would work as a peer to move the school to the next level of development.

By the early spring of 1999 Belvedere was on strong footing again, having weathered lost momentum and flagging spirits. The school possessed many of the features of high leadership capacity: broad-based, skillful participation; a shared vision; established norms of inquiry and collaboration; reflective practice; and improving student achievement. Jennifer became a rapt student of leadership, working closely with the principal and teacher and parent leaders. By the fall of 2000, she had entered the leadership preparation program at her local university.

In the summer of 2001, Principal Trevor decided to accept an assistant superintendency in a nearby district. The superintendent of Belvedere's district called Jennifer and asked her to pay him a visit; he wanted to see if she was interested in applying for the principalship. As honored as she was apprehensive, Jennifer listened as the superintendent asked her three questions:

- What have you learned about leadership?
- What have you learned about leadership capacity?
- Can you help sustain Belvedere's high leadership capacity?

What Is Leadership?

What *had* Jennifer learned about leadership?

"Leadership," she told the superintendent, "is about learning together toward a shared purpose or aim."

Learning and leading are deeply intertwined, and we need to regard each other as worthy of attention, caring, and involvement if we are to learn together. Indeed, leadership can be understood as reciprocal, purposeful learning in a community. Reciprocity helps us build relationships of mutual regard, thereby enabling us to become colearners. And as colearners we are also coteachers, engaging each other through our teaching and learning approaches. Adults as well as children learn through the processes of inquiry, participation, meaning and knowledge construction, and reflection (see Figures 1.1 and 1.2).

Figure 1.1 suggests ways of applying constructivist principles for teaching to the realm of leadership. As leaders, we must bear in mind the learners' views, challenge their beliefs, engage them in assessments that take into account the complexities of the broader context (e.g., leading beyond the classroom), and construct meaning and knowledge through

FIGURE 1.1

A Comparison of Constructivist Teaching and Leading

Constructivist teachers	Constructivist leaders
Seek and value students' points of view	Seek and value teachers' points of view
Structure lessons to challenge students' suppositions	Structure the concept of leadership to challenge teachers' belief systems
Recognize that students must attach relevance (meaning) to the curriculum	Construct meaning through reflection and dialogue
Structure lessons around big ideas, not small pieces of information	Structure the life of the school around the Big Picture, not a singular event or small piece of information
Assess student learning in the context of daily classroom investigations, not performances or isolated events	Assess teacher learning in the context of the complexity of the learning organization, not outcomes of isolated events

Note: Adapted from a paper by Janice O'Neil at the University of Calgary.

FIGURE 1.2
Parallels Between Teaching Habits of Mind and Leading

Activity	Teaching	Leading
Modeling	Modeling of what we want students to do. If we want students to be thoughtful, we need to demonstrate what thoughtfulness looks like.	Modeling of leadership behaviors. If we want others to be leaders, we need to demonstrate what leadership looks like.
Coaching	Helping students to think through what they are trying to do. The teacher raises questions rather than telling students what to do.	Helping others to think through what they are trying to do. Teachers raise questions with each other rather than telling others what to do.
Scaffolding	Providing the content bridges necessary for the task, raising the necessary questions, and giving students the opportunities to explore and perform the task.	Providing the content bridges necessary for the task, raising the necessary questions, and giving others, particularly new teachers, the opportunities to explore and perform the task.
Articulation	Explaining what the teacher is thinking about so that thinking is visible to the student.	Explaining what the teacher is thinking about so that thinking is visible to colleagues and parents.
Reflection	Being reflective and thoughtful about the work. Raising evaluation questions: What went well today? Why? If I did this again, how would I do it differently?	Being reflective and thoughtful about the work. Raising evaluation questions: What went well today? Why? If I did this again, how would I do it differently?
Exploration	Modeling risk taking so students understand that uncertainty is involved in all new learning.	Modeling risk taking so others understand that uncertainty is involved in all new learning.

Note: Adapted from Costa and Kallick (2000) and Lambert et al. (2002).

reflection and dialogue. Figure 1.2 draws parallels between teaching "habits of mind" (Costa & Kallick, 2000) and leading. These parallels suggest that leadership is the cumulative process of learning through which we achieve the purposes of the school.

As principals and teachers, we must attend not only to our students' learning but also to our own and to that of the adults around us. When we do this, we are on the road to achieving collective responsibility for the school and becoming a community of learners.

How we define leadership frames how people will participate in it. For instance, if we think of acts of leadership as "doing what the community needs when it needs to be done," they could include such simple tasks as inviting a new teacher to a meeting, raising a question that challenges established beliefs, or taking notes in an action research group.

Within the context of education, the term "community" has almost come to mean any gathering of people in a social setting. But real communities ask more of us than merely to gather together; they also assume a focus on a shared purpose, mutual regard and caring, and an insistence on integrity and truthfulness. To elevate our work in schools to the level required by a true community, then, we must direct our energies and attention toward something greater than ourselves.

When we learn together as a community toward a shared purpose, we are creating an environment in which we feel congruence and worth. Inherent to this view is the belief that all humans are capable of leadership, which complements our conviction that all children can learn. This vision of leadership asks that we keep in mind the following assumptions:

- Everyone has the right, responsibility, and capability to be a leader
- The adult learning environment in the school and district is the most critical factor in evoking acts of leadership
- Within the adult learning environment, opportunities for skillful participation top the list of priorities
- How we define leadership frames how people will participate in it
- Educators yearn to be purposeful, professional human beings, and leadership is an essential aspect of a professional life
- Educators are purposeful, and leadership realizes purpose

These assumptions determine our understanding of the work of leadership, which is integral to the definition of leadership capacity.

What Are We Learning About Leadership Capacity?

By "leadership capacity" I mean *broad-based, skillful participation in the work of leadership.* By "broad-based" I mean that if the principal, a vast majority of the teachers, and large numbers of parents and students are all involved in the work of leadership, then the school will most likely have a high leadership capacity that achieves high student performance.

But breadth of participation alone does not result in high leadership capacity; skillful involvement is needed as well. Otherwise our work together is unfocused, unproductive, and chaotic. Collaboration without skill is unsatisfying and will inevitably be abandoned for unilateral and thus more efficient ways of working. Collaboration that doesn't work can be a real setback, because it makes participants more hesitant to offer their time and commitment to working with others in the future. (I discuss the skills necessary for successful collaboration more fully in Chapter 3.)

Leadership capacity can refer to an organization's capacity to lead itself and to sustain that effort when key individuals leave; to the specific individuals involved; and to role groups, such as principals, teachers, parents and community members, and students. For the purposes of this book, however, I have focused my discussion primarily on leadership capacity as an organizational concept.

The combination of breadth of participation and depth of skillfulness gives rise to four possible organizational leadership capacity scenarios, as seen in Figure 1.3. Each quadrant in the figure includes a set of parallel features relating to the role of the principal, information and inquiry, program coherence, collaboration and

FIGURE 1.3
Leadership Capacity Matrix

	Low Degree of Participation	High Degree of Participation
Low Degree of Skill	• Principal as autocratic manager • One-way flow of information; no shared vision • Codependent, paternal/maternal relationships; rigidly defined roles • Norms of compliance and blame; technical and superficial program coherence • Little innovation in teaching and learning • Poor student achievement or only short-term improvements on standardized tests	• Principal as "laissez faire" manager; many teachers develop unrelated programs • Fragmented information that lacks coherence; programs that lack shared purpose • Norms of individualism; no collective responsibility • Undefined roles and responsibilities • "Spotty" innovation; some classrooms are excellent while others are poor • Static overall student achievement (unless data are disaggregated)
High Degree of Skill	• Principal and key teachers as purposeful leadership team • Limited use of schoolwide data; information flow within designated leadership groups • Polarized staff with pockets of strong resistance • Efficient designated leaders; others serve in traditional roles • Strong innovation, reflection skills, and teaching excellence; weak program coherence • Student achievement is static or shows slight improvement	• Principal, teachers, parents, and students as skillful leaders • Shared vision resulting in program coherence • Inquiry-based use of data to inform decisions and practice • Broad involvement, collaboration, and collective responsibility reflected in roles and actions • Reflective practice that leads consistently to innovation • High or steadily improving student achievement

responsibility, reflection, and student achievement. It is only when a school staff has undertaken skillful work using inquiry, dialogue, and reflection to achieve student performance goals that a school can be said to have achieved high leadership capacity (Quadrant 4).

The Features of Leadership Capacity

The features of each quadrant in Figure 1.3 relate to critical aspects of school improvement. Research and experience tell us that the characteristics in Quadrant 4 are prerequisites for high leadership capacity schools and organizations (Newmann & Wehlage, 1995).[1] I describe these criteria more fully in the chapters that follow, but below is a brief introduction to each.

Principals, Teachers, Parents, and Students as Skillful Leaders

Principals, teachers, parents, and students are the key players in the work of schooling. When working together, they form a concentration of leadership that is a powerful force in a school. If led by a skillful principal, teachers will often band together to form a team of professionals that invites parents and students into the work of leadership.

When individuals work together in reflective teams, they make the most out of their combination of talents. For instance, faculty meetings are occasions for educators to learn collaboratively, action research teams elicit inquisitiveness and a regard for evidence, and study groups test the assumptions of their members by introducing them to new ideas.

Shared Vision Resulting in Program Coherence

A principal's vision, standing alone, needs to be "sold" and "bought into." By contrast, a *shared* vision based upon the core values of participants and their hopes for the school ensures commitment to its realization. Realizing a shared purpose or vision is an energizing experience for participants, and a shared vision is the unifying force for participants working collaboratively.

_____

1. See also: Caplan, 1999; Conzemius and O'Neill, 2001; Kohm, 2002; Lambert, Walker, Zimmerman, Cooper, Gardner, M. Lambert, and Szabo, 2002; Pechura, 2001; Schmoker, 1996, 2002; Senese, 1999; and Spillane, Halverson, and Diamond, 2001.

Commitment to a shared vision provides coherence to programs and learning practices. Without coherence, wonderful classrooms operate next door to poor ones, and pioneering instructional practices under the same roof as ones that were long ago discredited. Every principal knows that parents will demand that their children be placed in the best classrooms with the best teachers. And who can blame them? We all want the best for our children. When quality stretches across the school's classrooms, curriculum, assessment, and instruction, we can provide equitable learning experiences for *all* children.

Inquiry-Based Use of Information to Inform Decisions and Practice

In a school that meets the criteria outlined in Quadrant 1 of the Leadership Capacity Matrix, information travels in a single direction—from the top to the bottom—without engaging in dialogue or negotiating new ways of thinking. A school that meets the criteria of Quadrant 4, however, provides a generative approach to discovering information and making collaborative, inquiry-based decisions. Questions are posed, evidence is collected and reflected upon, and decisions and actions are shaped around the collected findings. Outside information and formal research are mediated by the inquiry process. School community members understand that they are the primary leaders of the improvement process.

Information gleaned through inquiry informs both decisions and practice. Teachers frustrated by unruly students, bullying in the halls, or disrespectful classroom behavior, for example, will typically express their feelings in a faculty meeting. If the norm is to jump from the expression of opinions to action, then the faculty might simply decide to adopt a stricter discipline code. But if opinions lead to *inquiry* before action, a consideration of multiple voices, such as those of parents and students, might lead to efforts at building community in the classroom, mentoring students, or expanding student involvement in the school *in addition to* an examination of discipline codes.

BROAD INVOLVEMENT, COLLABORATION, AND COLLECTIVE RESPONSIBILITY REFLECTED IN ROLES AND ACTIONS

As individuals work together, their personal identities begin to change: principals expect colleagues to participate more fully, teachers find more efficient ways to do their work, and parents and students shift from seeing themselves as subjects to seeing themselves as partners. Collaboration and the expansion of roles lead to a sense of collective responsibility for all the students in the school, the broader school community, and the education profession as a whole. The more people who work collaboratively are able to experience their profession outside the school—through networks, conferences, professional organizations, etc.—the broader their scope of responsibility becomes. As a kindergarten teacher recently told me, "When I began this work as a teacher leader, I saw myself as a kindergarten teacher. Now I see myself as an educator." What she meant was that she was now ready, "as an educator," to assume responsibility for schoolwide improvements—and in her case specifically, for novice teachers and a university partnership.

REFLECTIVE PRACTICE THAT LEADS CONSISTENTLY TO INNOVATION

Reflective practice—that is, thinking about your own practice and enabling others to think about theirs—can be a source of critical information or "data." Practice here means how we do what we do—methods, techniques, strategies, procedures, and the like. Parents practice parenting; students practice learning and contributing to others; and teachers practice teaching, learn-

ing, and leading. Reflection enables us to reconsider how we do things, which of course can lead to new and better approaches to our work.

Strategies for reflection include writing about practice (in journals or otherwise), peer coaching, debriefing (of meetings, lessons, etc.), studying articles or books with peers, and reflecting on the results of student interviews. Reflection is our way of making sense of the world around us through metacognition.

HIGH OR STEADILY IMPROVING STUDENT ACHIEVEMENT

"Student achievement" in the context of leadership capacity is much broader than test scores. Measures of student achievement include multiple measures of development and performance, which in addition to test scores includes portfolios, exhibits, self-knowledge, and social maturity. This broad or comprehensive understanding of student achievement includes personal and civic development such as is involved in the work of "resiliency." Developmental factors of resiliency include: social bonding, opportunities to participate and contribute to others, problem-solving and goal-setting skills, and a sense of being in charge of one's future. Further achievement concerns are related to closing the yawning gap in achievement—typically derived from statistical measures such as test scores—among students of different genders, ethnicities, and socioeconomic statuses. At the heart of this problem are the differential skills and knowledge with which students enter and leave school. As a result, the average black or Latino student graduates from high school with the same skill set in math, reading, and vocabulary as a white 8th grader (Hammond, 1999). Each of these student-learning factors—academic performance, resiliency, and equitable outcomes for all students—is at the heart of leadership capacity; indeed, it is the compelling content of leadership.

Leadership Capacity Scenarios

The above features of leadership capacity are combined in each quadrant of Figure 1.3 to form a school "type." A caution: categories, types, and boxes are metaphors for our tendency to exist in a particular way. No school will or should "fit" exclusively into one quadrant. However, one can expect to find that a school has a tendency to function more in one way than another, signaled by a set of features that cluster together. This tendency to function at a particular level of leadership capacity is a changing, dynamic process.

THE QUADRANT 1 SCHOOL

Jennifer became dissatisfied with her original school, Creekside, when she realized that neither she nor her colleagues would be able to play a substantial role in achieving the mission of the school. Her efforts to become sufficiently well informed to make decisions about practice were thwarted by the school's top-down, one-way approach to disseminating information. Teachers were not expected to respond to the information they received—they would simply seek and either receive or be denied permission from the principal for most actions. Many teachers liked this "permissions-based culture," as it allowed them to blame any shortcomings on the decisions of others.

Teaching behaviors were similar throughout Creekside, reinforced by years of habit and lack of expectations for improvement. This uniformity of conduct could be interpreted superficially as indicative of the school's coherence (albeit in the service of the status quo) but Jennifer realized that a system of conforming to poor practice had little to recommend it.

Students who arrived at Creekside "ready to learn" did just fine. But teachers were resistant to assuming responsibility for those who had been poorly prepared in the previous grades,

lacked parent support, or were lax in doing what was required of them. The principal, busy with administrative work, chose not to challenge this culture of low expectations. Predictably, student performance was low. At one time, a new principal temporarily breathed some life into the school and the community witnessed a short-term rise in test scores, but that moment quickly came and went.

The major challenge of a Quadrant 1 school such as Creekside is to realign relationships in order to move from a hierarchical culture to a reciprocal one. Until relationships are shifted, dependency and blame will prevail.

THE QUADRANT 2 SCHOOL

Down the road from Creekside is the feeder high school for Belvedere, Sampson High. A lot goes on at Sampson, which is a comprehensive four-year school. Many students are involved in sports, theater, and the ROTC. The principal and assistant principal go to all the games and are respected in the community. Departments are managed by heads who have served in their roles for many years. Teachers have involved the students in community apprenticeships, a science and agricultural grant program, and a new technology venture that has enabled the school to start a computer lab.

Yet many students at Sampson are not involved in any activities, and in fact are barely thought of at all. Faculty meetings are short, held as needed, and consist only of announcements and business. Though broad, class offerings are uncoordinated—some might say fragmented—and department heads order new texts every five years or so. New teachers provided by the local university tend not to stay long unless they grew up in the community. Most students who don't drop out of Sampson get local jobs through apprenticeships, enter technical training, or go to the community college 18 miles away. About 12 percent go on to a four-year university.

The major challenge of a Quadrant 2 school such as Sampson is to create a sense of purpose—a unifying vision based on core values. This vision can help ensure that staff members confront the evidence of students "falling between the cracks" and develop quality programs to assist them.

THE QUADRANT 3 SCHOOL

At the time of Jennifer's transfer, Belvedere Middle School might have been described as a Quadrant 3 school. A leadership team worked with the principal to design reforms and make decisions based on school data. Many of the team members had used a reform network to hone their skills of reflection and collaboration. Several innovations—advisement, greater parent involvement, core curriculum with some team teaching, "untracking" of math—were on the drawing board, and student achievement was improving slightly.

But as time went on, polarization became more pronounced. Those who resisted the changes began to work against them; they felt that they had been isolated and even shunned by those in the leadership circle. When the principal left in the summer of 1998, these individuals took the opportunity to become more public with their views. By the fall, many anticipated initiatives had failed to materialize.

Eventually the school leaders came to understand what went wrong and shared their insights with Jennifer and the new principal. Teachers in leadership positions had chosen to ignore the quiet resistance of their colleagues for several reasons: some felt that a critical mass could be achieved without including those with serious questions, others felt that the resisters would eventually "see the light," and others still were uncomfortable with the possibility that conflict would surface if they opened the circle to everyone.

Jennifer learned that the major challenge of a Quadrant 3 school is to involve everyone in the reciprocal activities of collaborative leadership. Although adult conflict can be uncomfortable, it is essential to hear and try to understand opposing views in order for school improvement to be implemented schoolwide.

THE QUADRANT 4 SCHOOL

Two years into Jennifer's tenure, Belvedere had evolved into a Quadrant 4 school. The principal shared power skillfully with teachers, parents, community members, and students. Effective faculty meetings, a leadership team with a broad range of members, study groups, and vertical learning communities had created a collaborative environment where relationships could flourish and educators could sharpen their skills. Faculty members asked each other hard questions and provided one another with feedback, and adhering to collaborative norms became established procedure. Action research became routine: questions and concerns were subjected to thoughtful dialogue and thoroughly investigated. Peer coaching and reflective practices such as faculty writing and portfolios regularly resulted in novel approaches to problems. The role of teacher took on new meaning as collective responsibility extended to the school and community: teachers were now also change agents, coaches, facilitators, advisors, and mentors to students and new teachers.

Students found an engaging and supportive learning environment as well. Relationships developed with teachers and students evoked leadership. In focus groups, students reported that they felt valued as contributing members of the community. Student achievement rose across the board, and disaggregated data revealed that achievement gaps were closing.

The major challenge for Belvedere now is sustainability. As the current principal leaves and a new principal enters, the school will be challenged to maintain its momentum and quality. Similarly, new teachers will need to draw energy and wisdom from colleagues if they are to become full members of the leadership community.

In the pages that follow, we will examine the effect of leadership capacity on student and adult learning and on sustainable communities before engaging a more thorough discussion of the concept of sustainability.

Questions and Activities

Discuss in teams or with the whole faculty:

1. Do we believe that all teachers can lead? If so, what would this look like in our school?

2. Divide a paper into four quadrants. In teams of four to six, write four ways in which you learn best, one in each quadrant. Pass the sheet around to all members of the team until everyone has contributed. Discuss any patterns.

3. Identify the behaviors that you would observe in a good classroom. What would students and teachers be doing? Summarize your understandings of quality teaching and learning. How might you transfer those practices to your faculty meetings?

4. Examine Figure 1.3. Circle items that describe your school. Discuss your choices and identify possible areas for intervention.

5. Discuss any actions in your school that are related to one of the following four areas: participation, information/inquiry, collaboration, and program coherence. How might you increase the quality of your school's performance in this regard?

6. Turn to Appendix A and identify the chief challenges for your school. Read and discuss the recommended strategies for intervention. Add your own and discuss.

Chapter 2
Major Participation Patterns

Belvedere's transition from a Quadrant 3 to a Quadrant 4 school was due to deeper and more extended participation patterns and professional development practices. Those who felt left out of the dialogue within the school either did not actively participate in focused conversations or participated in a passive or abrasive manner, and had had few opportunities either inside or outside the school to learn how to participate in productive and meaningful ways. Meaningful participation, though a cornerstone of school communities, is often not emphasized nearly enough.

Still, meaningful participation is a cornerstone of professional and school communities—a stone that we often leave unturned. The first principle of participation is to ask whose voices are heard or generously represented. Are parents, teachers, students, community members,

administrators, and staff involved in important ways? Broad-based participation invites all stakeholders into the conversation.

Our attempts at "restructuring" during the past decade have left us somewhat disillusioned with the notion. This is unfortunate. Restructuring was intended to create avenues for people to be together so that they could get to know each other and build relationships, hold genuine dialogue, explore ideas together, and generally interact in productive, beneficial ways.

Participation patterns draw from the original intention of restructuring and make more explicit the above criteria. When we observe for patterns, we need to ask whether they

- Provide everyone with multiple opportunities for involvement,
- Are built around a shared vision,

- Involve opportunities designed for learning,
- Include norms that focus the conversation so that teams continually reflect on their behaviors,
- Include opportunities that are focused on the mission of the school, and
- Are skillfully facilitated.

As these criteria suggest, it is important to develop multiple ways for people to participate, and for each person to contribute in more ways than one. For instance, all faculty members participate in general faculty meetings—some in a leadership team, others in study groups, and others still in action research teams and learning communities. All members need to take part in an inquiry process based on data regarding student and adult performance. In so doing, they learn and draw meaning from diverse but related sources, and offer new insights of their own. (It is important to note here that the shared school vision is what keeps these insights congruent.) Ideally, the school will decide on a rich organizational pattern that brings everyone into more than one shared experience; for example, faculty meetings, vertical learning communities, and cross-school study groups could work in concert with one another. Interlocking patterns can maximize the effects of participation.

Preparing to Participate

"Readiness" refers to that which needs to be established or undertaken early in the participatory process. This is not meant to suggest a linear approach, however. Rather, the benefits of participation—improved relationships, altered assumptions and beliefs, shared goals and purposes, increased maturity and cognitive complexity—emerge in a spiraling way: the greater the participation, the greater the development; the greater the development, the higher the quality of participation.

The most powerful forms of participation are based on inquiry. In my research, I've witnessed many examples of inquiry-based participation in schools. One school sought to understand why the performance of Latina girls dropped after the 1st grade, another conducted focus groups with parents in order to understand their aspirations for their children and their expectations of the school, and another interviewed students to find out why homework was not being completed consistently and what could be done about it. Inquiry requires our natural inquisitiveness to surface, which can only occur when sufficient time and space are allotted for dialogue and critical questions. Trust is essential as well, and arises when people come to understand each other and decide that others can be counted on to act in ways consistent with personal and community values.

A few preparatory tasks can jump start the process of participation and contribute to greater success earlier in the process. One such task is the establishment of norms of behaviors within the adult community, which should be observed and reflected back to the group on a regular basis. Feedback can be corrective, allowing collegial observations to mirror group behavior back to the participants.

A process that I've found particularly useful for establishing norms is that of creating small teams within the larger group and asking each person to reflect upon a few characteristics of successful teams with which they have worked in the past. (I recommend small teams because they often prove particularly energizing and productive.) Each small team then considers every member's ideas and selects six to eight norms that are particularly meaningful to the whole staff. Typical norms include being respectful to each other, listening respectfully to all voices, prohibiting "sidebar" conversations, using dialogue on each agenda, clarifying processes for decision making, and designating responsibility for the implementation of group decisions.

Barbara Kohm, former principal of Captain Elementary School in Clayton, Missouri, described the school's five participatory norms, stated as questions:

- Did many people have a chance to lay out their thinking and receive feedback from colleagues?
- Did the topics directly connected to the everyday work of teachers and to the shared vision of the school receive ample time for discussion?
- Were there many opportunities for every voice to be heard?
- Was civil disagreement encouraged rather than glossed over?
- Did teachers leave the meeting with a deeper understanding of issues?

In addition to establishing norms, it is vital that team members get to know one another so that they can deepen their understanding of diverse views. One-on-one conversations, activities that reveal information about each other (such as exchanging one-page vitas), and opportunities to share past successes can build connections and context. Schools that systematically use faculty retreats understand the power of relationships. Concentrated time, such as during a retreat, can help build teams, relationships, and trust.

Participation Patterns

Perhaps the most common setting for participation is the general faculty meeting. We all know that poorly designed meetings can be deadly. Well-designed ones, on the other hand, can constitute an articulated series of learning experiences. Faculty meetings can be a major source of energy for the school when the following criteria are met:

- Community norms are clearly established
- The meeting is managed by a skilled facilitator and a process observer
- The agenda is focused on issues that genuinely affect teaching and learning practices
- Strategies are in place for distributing the work of the school among participants
- The agenda is developed by a leadership team; includes outcomes, processes, and responsibilities; allows for reflection, dialogue, inquiry, and action; and is distributed ahead of time
- Meetings are designed so that important issues and appropriate evidence can be thoughtfully examined

Conzemius and O'Neill (2001) describe several types of faculty gatherings—such as sequenced, result-oriented 30-minute meetings—that are focused and purposeful. They suggest five efficient, inquiry-based ways to achieve in-depth thinking and planning within reasonable time frames. They recommend that team members:

- Identify and isolate the gap between what is wanted and the current situation
- Identify specific, measurable, learner-focused goals for priority areas
- Correlate best practices to current practices
- Identify preferred staff development methods
- Analyze the results and refocus

TEAMING

Teams, like meetings, are essential to school participation. Many schools find it difficult to team successfully, however, because the process requires adults to organize and relate to one another in new ways. I often hear people say in exasperation that some teams work very well while others do not. Teams are too important to be left to chance. (I discuss the skills and insights essential for teams to function properly in Chapter 3.)

The **leadership team,** sometimes called the **site-management** or **learning support team,** is a vitally important design team for building leadership capacity. (The purpose of a design team is to create "lesson plans" for faculty gatherings, as with Conzemius and O'Neill's five recommendations.) The leadership team has historically been thought of as a surrogate decision-making team, in that it makes decisions for and on behalf of the staff and community. Figure 2.1 outlines suggested functions, responsibilities, and processes of leadership teams. The team broadens participation when it leverages opportunities for others to be involved. If the team makes decisions independent of an involved staff, we may see the polarization characteristics of a Quadrant 3 school.

EXAMPLES OF PARTICIPATION PATTERNS
FROM SCHOOLS AND DISTRICTS

The following examples of participation are from schools that are involved in building leadership capacity. Some of the designs are unique; others are adapted from established models and tailored to the needs and cultures of the school or district.

Members of **study groups** focus on reading and discussing articles or books. Educators in Alberta, Canada; Kansas City, Kansas; Clayton, Missouri; Columbus, Ohio; and San Leandro, California, regularly use study groups to challenge and integrate their thinking and reach new levels of understanding. Barbara Kohm explains that study groups began at her school as a way for educators to examine their assumptions about student learning:

> We read and discussed articles and books that presented different points of view about how children learn and how to organize learning experiences. As we read, talked, and sometimes argued with one another, we discovered that

some basic tenets on which we had built our practice were actually unexamined assumptions. For example:

- Children learn best when they are grouped with others of similar ability
- Intelligence is a fixed quantity present at birth
- Competition increases learning
- Some students are broken, and it's our job to fix them
- Learning is linear and takes place in an invariant sequence

From these unexamined assumptions, we had come to believe, for example, that students must learn phonics before they can read, spelling before they can write, and algorithms before they can reason mathematically (Kohm, May 2002).

Action research teams capture the essence of inquiry by endeavoring to learn more about compelling questions of practice, leading to new actions. Edie Brock, superintendent of the Seven Oaks school system in Manitoba, Canada, described to me how educators faced the press for student retention: because the school system had a culture of inquiry in place, staff members conducted a study to find out what happened later in life to individuals who had been retained in school. The study led to a district-published book; as a result of the staff members' research, Seven Oaks no longer retains students.

In the **vertical learning communities** of Kansas City, Kansas, multiple grades are linked together as a community and teaching assignments are "looped" (i.e., the teacher stays with a group of students for more than one year). These communities are able to develop long-term relationships with students, and are granted discretion on matters of instruction, discipline, and family outreach. Wyandotte High School, for example, has eight communities, each of which encompasses students from grades 9 to 12. The

FIGURE 2.1
Leadership Team Guidelines

Purposes of Leadership Teams

- Broadening the base of leadership in the school
- Paying thoughtful attention to the development of a professional learning community
- Modeling leadership for other members of the school community
- Focusing on student learning

Roles for Leadership Teams

- Designing professional learning opportunities in the school (including staff meetings, study groups, and action research)
- Establishing inquiry practices in the school (including the securing of evidence and data)
- Coordinating initiatives in alignment with the school's vision and goals
- Inviting leadership from others
- Communicating with and among members of the school community
- Paying attention to the development of the leadership skills of members
- Modeling leadership practice and skills

How to Establish Effective Leadership Teams

- Create readiness for a leadership team among staff by talking with individuals and groups, sharing readings, and discussing roles and responsibilities
- Clarify who will be accorded membership (e.g., classified staff? parents? students?)
- Carefully select members based on faculty criteria
- Convene and orient members to purposes, roles, and responsibilities; write and share clear by-laws, including a member rotation plan
- Establish initial responsibilities and calendar and assess needs for essential skills
- Organize responsibilities for facilitation and process observation
- Create team norms—expectations for working together
- Provide training in essential skills
- Establish a study process so that each meeting includes some new learning about a new idea, reading, skill, etc.
- Establish feedback loops so that school community communication is comprehensive and multi-leveled (e.g., each member is responsible for personal communication with a small group of staff)
- Create a team agenda process to address team roles
- Continually assess where you are, where you are going, and what you need

communities have the authority to develop schedules, handle advising and discipline, develop curriculum, and work with families on their own. To the extent possible, the same teacher stays with a student in a subject area throughout the student's four years of high school (Lambert et al., 2002).

The **vision team** at Hawthorne High School in Kansas City, Kansas, helps principal Jayson Strickland to analyze data and design, advocate, monitor, and implement the school improvement plan. Composed of representatives from various school departments (e.g., teachers from different grade levels, special education teachers, and reading specialists) who are nominated and selected by faculty, the team helps keep the plan alive and systematically implements its components during group planning time. Meetings are open to anyone who wants to attend. (The idea for the vision team originated with Donna Hardy, one of the four executive directors responsible for vertical learning communities in the district.)

The **Dreamkeepers** at Garfield School in San Leandro describe their team as "a volunteer group of staff members who consciously keep equity at the forefront of their minds and in all of their personal and professional actions, while remaining committed to ensuring that it is not forgotten in the minds of others." Principal Jan Huls further notes that the group is fluid, with open membership. Frequent retreats and regular meetings enable the team members to design curriculum units and instructional practices, as well as share ideas and research literature on equity.

At Maple Ridge School in Calgary, Canada, routine leadership tasks are distributed using the **ZCI process** (see Figure 2.2). Under this system, "Z" (for "authorized") refers to the person or people responsible for a task, "C" stands for those who wish to be consulted, and "I" stands for those who wish to be informed. Ad hoc

groups are formed to do the routine work of the school, thereby preserving precious faculty meeting time for in-depth dialogue. Leadership teams, learning support teams, school councils, and vision teams are other ways to organize for the purpose of designing participation patterns, thus setting the vital groundwork for decision making.

Curriculum teams were formed in Manitoba's Rhineland school system when the province mandated a standards-based curriculum. The top-down initiative might have taken power away from the school system, but Assistant Superintendent Dorothy Braun helped establish strong implementation teams by providing them with discretion, resources, support, and time. Consequently the teams became energized, teacher leadership increased, and inquiry was able to flourish. When teachers compared the current curriculum content to the content they desired, they were able to identify gaps in their knowledge, which led to investigation and experimentation. According to Braun, this was a real turning point. Study became inquiry, with teachers raising their own questions and helping each other to find solutions.

The Chief Justice Milvain School in Calgary, Canada, is a diverse elementary school of 460 children, 50 percent of whom are ESL students. Led by a group of teacher leaders known as the **Circle of Leaders,** the school developed an inquiry-based improvement plan using Understanding by Design. The process of developing the plan involved a broad leadership base of teachers, parents, and administrators; professional development with study groups; and dialogue, through which educators challenged their own assumptions about student learning and inquiry. The plan focused on four main objectives:

- Building a learning community
- Teaching for understanding

FIGURE 2.2
Maple Ridge Elementary School ZCI Chart of Staff Responsibilities

TOPICS	Z (authorized to assume major responsibility)	C (want to be consulted)	I (want to be informed)
Supervision Schedule	Carol, Peter, Janice	Joyce, Nancy, Elaine, Mary Lou	Schedule to all
Budget	Annette, Kelly, Carol L	Lorie, Julie, Linda, Lynn	all
Alberta Teachers Assoc.	Peter		all
Alberta Education	Provincial program	Elaine	all
Art	Lynn	Joyce, Patti, Linda	all
Calendar	Joyce, Janice, Carol L	Linda, Nancy	all
Clubs	Linda, Christine	Julie, Janice	all
Drama	Joyce, Julie, Linda		Schedule to all
ESL	Dianne	Elaine	all
Fine Arts Council	Nancy, Carol, Julie	Janice, Patti, Linda	all
Guidance	Carol, Dianne		All involved
Health	Mary Lou, Linda, Nancy, Patti	Janice, Elaine, Linda	all
Kindergarten	Lorie		all
Language Arts—Div. I	Joyce, Mary Lou, Christine	Janice, Dianne, Linda	all
Language Arts—Div. II	Learning community	Elaine, Patti, Dianne	all
Math	Nancy	Linda	all
Music & Concerts	Julie	Nancy, Linda	all
Outdoor Education	Bob		all
Phys. Ed.	Bob	Peter	all
Prof. Dev. Days	Lynn, Mary Lou, John, Lorie	Julie, Elaine, Linda	all
Science	Joyce, Peter, Patti	Julie, Patti, Linda	all
Social Studies	Linda	Julie, Elaine	all
Technology	Carol	Linda	all
Special Needs	Kathy L	Lorie, Dianne	all
Terry Fox program	Peter, Christine	Janice	all
Artist in Residence	Julie	Julie	all
Service Club	Bob, Carol L		all
Peer Support	Bob, Paul, Peter, Sandi		All involved
Assemblies and Special Events	Julie, Linda, Christine	Nancy	Schedule to all
Sports Day	Linda, Bob, John, Christine, Janice	all	
Student Council	Lynn, Lorie	Lorie, Janice, Nancy	all
Social Committee, Gifts, etc.	Janice, Lorie, Kathy L, Christine	Patti, Lynn, Linda	all
Parent Council	Janice, Mary Lou	Patti, Carol	all

- Representing, assessing, and responding to the implementation of Understanding by Design
- Access to and management of resources

The result was a remarkable plan that included all the features of high leadership capacity in a unique and integrated design.

The approaches to participation discussed above are most powerful when combined in a thoughtful and integrated school improvement process, such as at the Chief Justice Milvain School. Another good example is the approach of the Eden Gardens School in Hayward, California. Principal Rosalinda Canlas describes that school's involvement with the Bay Area School Reform Collaborative (BASRC):[1]

> Our staff and the school learning community take the business of educating our students very seriously. Our primary goal focuses our energy into addressing the needs of *all* of our students, especially those falling below grade level; we are bridging the gap between students who are currently achieving and those who fall in the bottom quartile. How do we do this? What teaching practices should teachers use to help students achieve?
>
> Eden Gardens' staff lives and breathes these big questions. Wednesday collaboration days are rotated among
>
> 1. The cycle of inquiry,
> 2. Action research,
> 3. Grade level meetings,
> 4. New teacher support meetings, and
> 5. Parent/community involvement.

---

1. BASRC, an Annenberg-Hewlett initiative in the San Francisco Bay Area, employs many of the strategies for building leadership capacity. The schools involved have developed strong professional cultures focused on ensuring that all children learn well.

During these collaborations, multiple assessment data help us find patterns that inform our instruction. Teacher leaders and the entire staff take responsibility for inquiring about the problem; researching possible solutions, answers and inventions; and implementing recommendations. During the dialogues and reflections, peers support each other in becoming more effective at teaching (personal communication, 2002).

Engaging Reluctant Teachers

Teachers participate in the above opportunities because it is interesting and rewarding to do and it is an expectation of their professional culture. A major assumption in the development of leadership capacity is that teachers yearn to be more fully who they are: purposeful, professional human beings. Of course, yearning alone won't help. Teachers often say that they don't see themselves as leaders, a self-assessment that in my view arises from old definitions of leadership as tied to role, position, and formal authority. When we define leadership as reciprocal, purposeful learning in a community, teachers are much better able to see the many opportunities for them to contribute.

Many teachers who say that they would prefer not to participate have either not had meaningful opportunities to do so, or have participated more fully previously in their careers only to be disappointed or discouraged when the work that they gave their hearts to was never implemented or sustained.

Full participation is first and foremost a function of design. When we design our times together as we would a powerful lesson, we include strategies that engage everyone, such as small group dialogue, cooperative learning strategies, problem solving, gallery walks, and protocol (see Chapter 3 for a more thorough discussion of this last term). Participation is also a matter of interest and will: educators need to see a close connection between what they value and the tasks at hand. This is why it is so important to use a shared vision as the guidepost for building leadership capacity.

When trying to get reluctant teachers to participate in the work of leadership, we should ask ourselves the questions in Figure 2.3. Notice that working through conflict is an important aspect of this endeavor. Often, those in the inner circle of leadership tend to ignore or avoid those who do not agree with the direction of the school. Confronting differences through personal conversation and deliberate interactions can enable us to find common ground.

Going to Scale

In reform communities, "going to scale" means enlarging the circle of participation to include everyone, or at least a much larger portion of the school or district community than was previously involved. To accomplish this, educators often must open up more opportunities for participation, redesign existing opportunities as interactive learning experiences, maintain an inclusive vision, and work through resistance to change. Such actions may involve slowing down for a period of time to engage in wider and deeper conversations.

FIGURE 2.3

Engaging Reluctant Teachers: Questions to Ask Ourselves

- How well do I really know this person's aspirations, values, history, and interests? Respect and trust grow from relationships.

- How well do our community norms of practice frame our behaviors together as a group?

- To what extent have we developed participation patterns around our professional work, such as using dialogue and evidence to focus on student learning?

- What opportunities for personal goal setting and learning have we made available so that individual interests and passions can be linked to school and district goals?

- How accessible and equitable is information, including resource information?

- How often and in what ways have I genuinely asked this individual for advice and consultation?

- Have we created feedback loops that involve the multidirectional flow of personal, written, and online information?

- When new things are added to your plate, what is removed to make room for them?

- How well do I use questions that evoke reflection, evidence observed, and inferences about own practice, whether in conversation or when coaching?

- Have we diminished "adoptions" in favor of school- and district-generated programs based on direct evidence and best practices?

The Relationship of Participation to Skillfulness: Structure and Process

As we saw in Chapter 1, the relationship between level of participation and degree of skillfulness is at the core of the framework for leadership capacity. It is what people learn and do together, rather than what any particular leader does alone, that creates the fabric of the school. Spillane, Halverson, and Diamond (2001) refer to the performance of these collaborative tasks as *task enactment*, a useful expression for understanding the patterns of interaction at the heart of leadership capacity. If participation patterns constitute the *structure* of leader capacity, skilled task enactment constitutes the *process*. Without such a dynamic relationship, school is like soft tissue, apt to melt away when key individuals leave.

Though participation is one of the key deciding factors, leadership capacity becomes fully realized only when the participants themselves become skillful. We have all been involved with decision-making groups that were actually rubber stamps. Most of us have experienced poorly conceived committee or faculty meetings. Many of us have committed to tasks only to have them overturned by an administrator. These are examples of contrived participation patterns devoid of skillfulness. High leadership capacity requires both.

Questions and Activities

Discuss in teams or with the whole faculty:

1. Using the processes described in this chapter, design an agenda for the staff meeting to develop community norms. Distribute and post.

2. Working with your leadership team or your whole staff, assess the level of participation in your school. How broad is it? Is everyone involved? In what ways?

3. Have your leadership team read and discuss Figure 2.1 (Leadership Team Guidelines).

4. How does your understanding of your team relate to these ideas? Are there guidelines here that would strengthen your team?

5. At the end of your next staff meeting, recruit a small group of staff members (or one of your existing teams) to help the principal design the next staff meeting agenda. Attend to the criteria described in this chapter.

6. Have any staff members at your school been reluctant to participate fully? Ask yourself the questions in Figure 2.3 (Engaging Reluctant Teachers). How might you work through any reluctance in order to go to scale?

7. Discuss the examples of different participation patterns presented in this chapter and compare them with the ones at your school.

CHAPTER 3
The Professional Development of Leaders

In the previous chapter, I described participation patterns as a means of bringing people together in new ways. But being together is not in and of itself a basis for success in schools.

Discussion during unskilled collaborative time tends to focus on two main topics: individual problem students and instructional materials and activities. Fortunately, most teachers now recognize the need to focus on seeking outcomes equitably for all students. To do this, we must know the quality of our students' work as well as the standards of performance, and learn how to facilitate adult conversations about those topics. Teachers and other staff members must perform as leaders in their communities, understand that the leadership of adults and the leadership of students are parallel concepts, and design professional development around the skillfulness to achieve leadership in and out of the classroom.

As noted in Chapter 1, it is vital that teachers and staff members understand the linkage between learning with students in the classroom and learning with colleagues. When teachers learn to facilitate faculty dialogue, they become better at facilitating classroom dialogue; when they listen well to colleagues, they pay the same degree of attention to their students; when they reflect aloud with colleagues, they enable students to reflect aloud; and when they expect to discover evidence to inform their own thinking, they begin to expect students to do the same on the path to problem solving and understanding.

Similarly, it is important for educators to recognize the connection between our own learning and that of our colleagues. When we think in terms of reciprocity, we understand that we are responsible for our own and our colleagues' learning as well as that of our students. This mutuality is at the heart of professional development.

Professional Development as "Opportunities to Learn"

It is currently common to tie professional development to specific student outcomes—say, "to improve sight recognition of words among 1st graders by 40 percent before the end of the year." In this example, professional development might accordingly be focused on skills for teaching sight recognition of words. This is a defensible and rational approach, given our focus on student learning. But it may ignore the fundamental truth that working together as adults is skillful work as well, and should not to be skipped over in our rush for quick results in test scores.

Though it is often used to mean simply "teacher training," I would define professional development to include learning opportunities that can be found in collegial conversations, coaching episodes, shared decision-making groups, reflective journals, parent forums, or other such occasions. Indeed, because the focus of such conversations may well be on a given discipline or skill—literacy, for instance, or problem solving—the learning of both teachers and students can be addressed concurrently.

Professional development designs that attend to both teacher and student learning might use what I refer to as the "reciprocal processes of constructivist learning." By this I mean learning that is mutual and interactive, thereby investing in the growth of all participants. The process includes the following activities:

- **Surfacing** of ideas, assumptions, histories, and prior knowledge: What do we currently believe and do?

- Engaging in **inquiry** (e.g., examining student work, conducting action research and observations, and reading and discussing recent research): What new knowledge can we generate?
- Entering into **dialogue** and **reflection** that we can understand: How do we make sense of prior assumptions and practice in light of what we now know?
- **Reframing** actions and plans to account for what we now know and understand: How will we reshape our practice and our school plan?

The highlighted words in the description above hold special significance. Leaders at the UCLA School Management program have found that reflection, inquiry, and dialogue are the three most critical skill dimensions for improving schools (Martinez, 2001). I heartily agree: most leadership skills flow from these three fundamental processes. Reflection, inquiry, and dialogue are interdependent—no one of them stands alone—and together they form the primary dynamic of professional practice. They occur effectively when educators collaborate together.

REFLECTION

Without reflection, it is possible to teach a single year 30 times over. Reflection—thinking about what we do before, during, and after our actions—is our cognitive guide for growth and development, a way of thinking that we should engage in continuously. Yet it is not unusual to hear people say they don't have the time to reflect. We can make reflection habitual by setting time aside specifically for this purpose: coaching, dialogue, journaling, questioning, self-assessment, and the use of personal professional development plans all encourage participants to reflect on their work. Such habits of practice become habits of mind.

INQUIRY

Inquiry skills enable us to transform our inquisitiveness into practice. We learn to inquire when we:

- Transpose a condition into a question for examination. If children are misbehaving, we should ask, "How can we help children to behave?"; if parents are not involved enough, "What are the best ways to get parents involved?"
- Coach for specificity using "inquiry coaching." (See Figure 3.1.)
- Collect evidence to address questions. Although the process of inquiry may begin either by examining data or by asking questions, the latter approach will result in more sustainable inquiry.
- In study groups, pose questions that arise from dialogue about research. This will unearth curiosities that in turn will nurture inquiry.

DIALOGUE

Dialogue is all too often absent in schools. Most school discussions revolve around a few dominant voices expressing their own points of view, with others chiming in to offer their opinions. The goal in such cases seems to be the dominance of one set of ideas over another. True understanding is a rare commodity when we are busy rehearsing and imparting our own opinions. Discussion that remains at this level is the result of unskillful meeting design, facilitation, and participation.

The purpose of dialogue is understanding: when we truly listen and build on each other's ideas, we construct meaning and knowledge together. I have found the guidelines in Figure 3.2 to be particularly useful for constructing productive dialogues. Time is precious in schools, so boundaries need to be set for most such discussions; I suggest somewhere between 20 minutes and one hour. Because dialogue demands a high level of skill, it needs to be

FIGURE 3.1
Inquiry Coaching: Finding the Question Together

The purpose of inquiry coaching is to identify, clarify, and focus a question for inquiry. Ask the questions below in pairs, small groups, or teams.

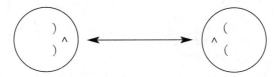

In coaching pairs, ask the following types of questions:

- **Describing:** "Tell me about the issue you are pondering."
- **Clarifying:** "Are all your students tardy? Which teachers do you think are reluctant leaders?"
- **Mediating:** "How do you interpret this situation?"
- **Concluding:** "What more would you like to know? What question do you have?"

facilitated and observed. Successful facilitation should maintain focus, include all voices, and move the agenda along by synthesizing and summarizing what has been said. A process observer should attend to the actions and interactions of the group and offer feedback based on adherence to dialogue guidelines.

The **protocol** is another form of reflective conversation that can be used to achieve goals similar to those of dialogue. Originally developed by the Coalition of Essential Schools, the protocol is currently used in schools throughout the United States and Canada. Its power lies in the use of reflective teams, genuine listening, critical thinking, and feedback. As can be seen in Figure 3.3, teachers at James Short Memorial Elementary School in Calgary use the protocol to examine research on literacy and how it applies to their own classroom practice. Educators at Sir Winston Churchill High School, also in Calgary, have used the protocol with curriculum leaders in order to examine their philosophies regarding education, with the staff as a whole during a professional development day, and even in the classroom. Both staff members and students report that more voices are heard, more listening occurs, and a deeper

understanding of the issues emerges when the protocol is used.

Teaming and Leadership Development

Teaming is perhaps the most challenging format for skillful leadership work. For one thing, successful teaming rests on the capacities of individuals to form relationships that enable them to work well together. It is not surprising to hear a principal wonder: "What do I do about my kindergarten team? One person dominates, one is passive, and one is continually in conflict with the dominant member." Surprisingly, we often tolerate a degree of ineffectiveness among adults that we would never tolerate among children, perhaps because we lack appropriate strategies for developing skillful adult participation.

To make teaming less dependent on member personalities, we need to situate it within a professional framework of skillful leading. In Chapter 2 I discussed how community norms and meeting agendas relate to teaming. In this chapter, I will explore two additional design features: roles and skills.

Roles

Role designations in teams are much like those in cooperative learning: there is a facilitator, a recorder, and a process observer. Each participant needs to be skilled in the following areas in order to successfully perform his role:

- Developing shared visions
- Facilitating group processes
- Communicating (listening/questioning)
- Reflecting on practice
- Inquiring about issues confronting the school community
- Using evidence to improve practice
- Engaging in collaborative planning

Figure 3.2
Guidelines for Dialogue

- Choose a facilitator and a process observer
- Attend to the "third thing in the room" (i.e., a question, quote, or poem, etc.)
- Listen carefully
- Ask probing questions
- Unmask assumptions
- Make connections and construct meanings
- Consider process feedback

FIGURE 3.3

Protocol—a Professional Reflective Conversation
for James Short Memorial Elementary School

Developing Shared Understandings Around Literacy Programming

Members of one team will function as "presenters" of their article, while those in the other team act as "reflectors" or "critical friends," asking questions and giving critical feedback.

Each team had its own article to read ahead of time.

INQUIRY QUESTIONS: Is our literacy instruction an example of thoughtful work? What might we also need to be thoughtful about?

Step	Time	Task
1.	8'	Team A: discuss the main points in your article briefly. *[Team B members listen <u>silently</u> and take notes.]*
2.	10'	Team B members ask <u>short clarifying</u> questions about the Team A article. *[Team A members give <u>short clarifying</u> responses.]*
3.	10'	Team A members discuss their article in more detail. They focus on how it affects their thinking about their classroom practice, and how it affects their thinking about the school's literacy work. *[Team B members listen <u>silently</u> and take notes.]*
4.	10'	Team B members talk among themselves about what they heard Team A say. They frame probing questions, share reactions, and formulate feedback and suggestions. *[Team A members listen <u>silently</u> and take notes.]*
5.	8'	Team A members discuss the feedback which they have just received by listening to Team B. They discuss feedback among themselves. *[Team B is silent.]*
6.	12'	Team A and B now conduct an open dialogue on the connections and insights they have made.

Reprinted by permission.

- Managing conflict among adults
- Problem solving and challenging colleague beliefs and assumptions
- Managing change and transitions
- Developing constructivist learning designs.

More specifically, teaming involves the following processes:

- Team members get to know one another's strengths and needs and accept that different members have different perspectives, interests, and strengths. Some schools use forms of the Myers-Briggs Type Indicator—such as "Colors" (Reynolds, 2002), "Creative Roles" (von Oech, 1986), and "The Four Hats of Leadership" (Garmston & Wellman, 1999)—to understand each other better.

- Teams maximize the use of each member's strengths. For example, one person might have a knack for data analysis, while another excels at planning; each person takes the lead responsibility in his area of strength.
- Teams are reciprocal learning communities in which each member expects to learn from and contribute to the development of the others.
- Key roles are selected based on the understanding that they will rotate and allow team members to become more skillful in the classroom. Members clarify team roles within each decision-making structure of the school.
- Team members develop shared goals and products (including performances, such as exhibitions of student work), as this helps to build professional relationships.
- Personal conflicts are not allowed to simmer. Team members employ a conflict resolution process—whereby they listen to each position, seek common ground, and identify strategies to address the problem—and call in a mediator if needed.
- Team members reflect upon and analyze each group session and seek ways to improve the team. Analysis begins with the process observer's report on how community norms were observed during the meeting. Members contribute their personal impressions.
- Team members network frequently with members of other teams in the school—during time built into staff meetings, for example—as well as with teams in other schools.

Leadership Perspective

Jennifer brought a "leadership perspective" to the task of learning to be a leader at Belvedere. Such a perspective requires an initial formulation of what leadership entails—among other things, learning with, contributing to, and influencing the learning of colleagues. A leadership perspective also requires us to watch for and codify leadership behavior: to notice, for instance, what questions are being asked (and what their effects are), what design features are suggested (and what their intended outcomes are), and what feedback is given (and what its purpose and effect is). Reflecting on these behaviors allows us to better understand what we have observed.

How Jennifer Learned to Be a Leader

Jennifer watched intently as the new principal and the teachers at Belvedere practiced leading. She participated in several modes of interaction, including leadership-team meetings and retreats, faculty meetings, study groups, and an action research team. In doing so she tried out her emerging skills, taking turns as a facilitator, process observer, critical questioner, and involved participant. It soon became a habit for Jennifer to design meetings thoughtfully and to reflect upon and debrief them afterwards. She found this process to be very much like lesson planning.

Jennifer's study group read and discussed *Building Leadership Capacity in Schools* (Lambert, 1998), followed by Garmston and Wellman's *The Adaptive School* (1999), a sourcebook that details the processes of leading and learning. Jennifer found instructional and leadership coaching, which became a regular feature of the school, to be a mutual exchange of ideas and observations; she realized that each time she was coached, she was coaching as well. Reflection was built into the life of the school through coaching, questioning, and journaling. She and others arranged for the whole faculty to be trained in inquiry and dialogue.

In the fall of 2000, Jennifer entered the nearby university to seek formal preparation in educational leadership and secure an administrative credential. As a result of the cohort arrangement at the university, which allowed her access to multiple sources of knowledge and deepened her understanding of the theory underlying good practice, Jennifer accelerated her learning and was moved to pursue a principalship.

Jennifer paid attention to her learning at Belvedere; she was alert to what others were doing and thinking as well as to what she was thinking and experiencing. Principal Trevor drew her attention to the leadership perspective and often coached her by asking what she was noticing and experiencing about her emerging role as a leader. This kind of attention is essential for "job-embedded" professional development (also known as "leadership task enactment"), whereby skills are learned primarily on the job rather than in a training session. Jennifer participated in experiences that called on her to think in new ways about working with colleagues—about teaming, designing, facilitating, analyzing, and debriefing. She experienced coaching from the new perspective of mutuality and reciprocity.

Jennifer synthesized the research she read in study groups and at the university with her current knowledge, and made sense of them in ongoing dialogues with colleagues. She also recognized that some skills needed to be directly taught because they were relatively new to the school and could be more effi-

ciently learned through training. Reflection on practice enabled her to weave her new knowledge into her work.

Developing Skillful Leadership: Examples from Practice

Most schools and districts rely on the effectiveness of job-embedded approaches to develop leadership skills. Here are a few examples:

- Anita Hayward at Hanna Ranch Elementary School, in California's West Contra Costa School District, designs staff meeting agendas around the reciprocal processes of constructivist learning. Although these agendas are primarily focused on students and student work, they teach educators leadership skills in the process. Schools with leadership capacity construct meeting agendas that model and teach leadership skills by specifying outcomes, roles, topics, processes, and observations.
- Every Wednesday at Garfield Elementary School in San Leandro, California, teachers take turns leading teams and all-staff professional development sessions in discussions of teaching practices and student work. Every time the teams meet, they complete a communiqué that informs the school of their activities, needs, and accomplishments. Teachers learn to facilitate different teams and capture the key ideas of each session for the school community.
- At Highland Park High School in Highland Park, Illinois, the entire staff is organized into learning teams of two to six teachers. These teams choose their own members, subjects to research, and methods of sharing information with the rest of the community. Assistant Principal Joseph Senese also describes an Action Research Laboratory (ARL) that operates side-by-side with the learning teams, for

teachers and administrators who want to conduct more in-depth action research. ARL participants receive more support and professional development and are allotted more time for research than the learning teams, and are in turn expected to disseminate their conclusions through publications and presentations and by serving as resources to the learning teams. Teachers and students at the school told me that the ARL helps them to advance the practices of collaboration, experimentation, and reflection.

- Because the teachers at Richmond High School in the West Contra Costa School District decided that successful facilitation made them better teachers and participants and more skillful at working with colleagues, the school improvement team arranged for facilitation training during winter and summer breaks. More than a third of the 100 faculty members are now skilled facilitators.

These school experiences were designed with three main goals in mind: accomplishing the school's mission, establishing structures in which educators can lead, and improving the leadership capabilities of the staff. Such designs emerge from an assessment and understanding of the school's leadership capacity. There are several ways, some formal and some informal, for undertaking such an assessment.

Assessing Leadership Capacity Skills and Understandings

Formal assessment tools have the advantage of focusing the school conversation on survey indicators related to leadership capacity while providing new data about the skillfulness of the staff and the actions of the whole. These instruments are designed to be used in four ways:

1) As self-assessment tools for professional development planning;
2) As colleague-assessment tools (e.g., teacher-to-teacher or teacher-to-administrator) in order to receive feedback for professional development planning from others;
3) As school-assessment tools, by compiling responses into a school profile that can pinpoint intervention spots for improvement planning (see the Lakemoor School example below); and
4) As training tools, to build familiarity with the concepts in the instruments.

I have included four tools for measuring leadership skills in the appendix. These tools are not, however, designed to be used for performance evaluation.

Assessment Tools

Appendixes B (the Rubric of Emerging Teacher Leadership) and C (the Continuum of Emerging Teacher Leadership) outline the different stages of leadership capacity development. In the rubric, each column corresponds to the different quadrants of the Leadership Capacity Matrix in Chapter 1. The continuum delineates the differences between reflective practitioners and teacher leaders who encourage others to practice reflection. (Notice that the major difference is that reflective practitioners who are not teacher leaders primarily enable themselves, while those who are leaders also focus on developing leading behaviors in others.) The rubric and continuum are best used as self-assessment and conversational tools in faculty meetings, teams, and coaching pairs. I use the rubric to identify teacher leadership skills; both it and the continuum can be used to develop leadership coaching.

Appendix D (the Leadership Capacity Staff Survey) includes items and indicators related to the features of high leadership capacity schools.

Item B of the survey enumerates the specific skills and understandings needed for developing leadership capacity. This tool, along with the continuum in Appendix C and the school survey in Appendix E, can be used to assess the professional development needs of both individuals and groups. The staff survey can be used in faculty or team meetings as well as with individuals. The summary on the last page of the survey forms a profile of the respondent's strengths and needs, each of which has implications for professional development. (The survey can also be used to launch a dialogue: for instance, I might ask participants to select any items concerning, say, inquiry, and to discuss ways in which such items connect with and reinforce each other.)

Appendix E (the Leadership Capacity School Survey) takes a broader look at the school as a whole, emphasizing the school as a cultural entity and recognizing that the whole is greater than the sum of its parts. This survey lends itself to faculty and team meetings and can lead to conversations about whole-school improvement. The summary box on the last page allows staff members to compare possible and actual scores, thereby noting the desired direction and quality of growth.

Figure 3.4 displays a bar graph developed from the summary box of the Leadership Capacity School Survey of Lakemoor Middle School. After taking the survey, Lakemoor staff members made the following observations:

- Because the school lacked a vibrant shared vision, the work of the different teams tended to be uncoordinated.
- Uses of inquiry were limited by a singular focus on standardized test scores.

FIGURE 3.4
Lakemoor Middle School Leadership Capacity Bar Graph

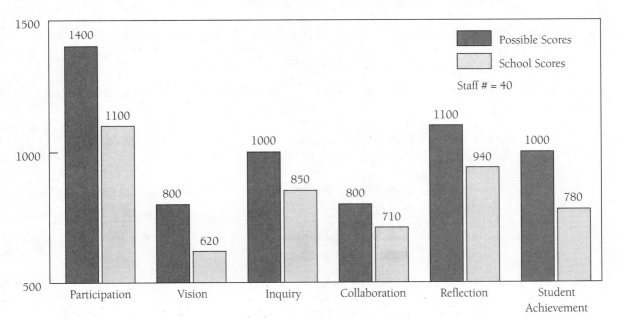

- Collaboration worked fairly well, but by restricting it to grade-level teams alone, the school created limited opportunities for collective responsibility.
- Although student performance was satisfactory on average, staff members should begin disaggregating data to better identify students who fall through the cracks.

Collaborative reflection on the survey raised the staff members' awareness of how to intervene collectively in their school, and encouraged them to view the school as a whole and work jointly to accomplish its mission.

The questions in Figure 3.5 can provide schools with a less formal and more flexible assessment process by presenting the key features of leadership capacity as open-ended questions. These questions have been used in focus groups, leadership team meetings, and whole-faculty conversations, as well as in individual surveys and in combination with other instruments (although they are most informative when used in an interactive setting). Each tool can provide vital information for the purposes of developing professional development processes and designing participation to enhance and expand leadership capacity.

FIGURE 3.5
School Assessment Questions

1. Do you have opportunities to participate in leadership at this school? Give an example.

2. How skillful do you feel you are in your collaborative work with colleagues? What are your areas of strength? Areas for growth?

3. Do we work together collaboratively? If so, please offer examples.

4. Are the purpose and core values of our school clear? How would you personally describe them?

5. How do we use data to improve student development and performance?

6. How do you think we are doing with regard to student performance? What added value do we bring to students' lives?

7. Can you think of an occasion when we have posed our own questions and sought our own answers about teaching and learning?

8. Are there other opportunities for reflective practice (such as coaching, writing, and dialogue) that we might look into?

9. What principal actions have encouraged and supported the above work? In what ways has the district supported our efforts to build leadership capacity?

10. As you reflect upon these questions, are there other comments that you would like to add?

Conclusion

So far in this book I have discussed high leadership capacity as a function of broad-based, skillful participation in the work of leadership—participation that naturally relies on the leadership qualities of the principal, teachers, staff, students, parents, and community members. By contributing energy and wisdom to a school or district, these voices help build sustainable school improvement. In the chapters that follow, I will focus on each of these groups of participants and discuss how the members of each can belong to a leadership community.

Questions and Activities

1. Think about how you became skillful in your own practice. How did you acquire your skills? How do you continue to learn about your work? What are the implications of your experience for professional development? Discuss.

2. How is professional development defined in your school? How might you refine the definition of professional development in your school? Connect your responses to your answers to Question 1 and to the ideas in this chapter.

3. This chapter makes the case that being a better teacher leader means becoming a better teacher. Discuss in small groups.

4. Design and convene a faculty meeting as a professional development experience using the reciprocal processes of constructivist learning presented in this chapter. After the meeting, debrief and reflect on the experience.

5. Consider the story of how Jennifer learned to be a leader. How many different forms of learning does her story include so far?

6. Distribute the staff and school surveys in Appendixes D and E a few days before a staff meeting so that staff members have time to read them beforehand. At the meeting, divide into groups of three to five and redistribute the survey. Ask everyone to complete it and tally the score. On a large piece of chart paper, display the results as a graph. Return to the small groups and focus the dialogue by asking what the data reveal about the leadership capacity of your school. Discuss. For the next meeting, prepare to ask staff members how they can intervene in the school's processes to develop stronger leadership capacity.

7. Convene focus groups of faculty, staff, students, and parents, either in mixed or role-specific groups. Distribute the assessment questions in Figure 3.5, explaining the purpose and meaning of the questions in relationship to the leadership capacity of the school. Ask the questions one at a time, allowing for dialogue and brief writing time after each one. Record group responses and ask each participant to record both group and personal responses. Collate the data and present it at a staff meeting for interpretation.

CHAPTER 4

Teachers as Leaders:
The Heart of the High Leadership Capacity School

Teachers who choose the path of teacher leadership . . . become owners and investors in their schools, rather than mere tenants.

—Roland Barth (1999)

All people yearn for vitality and purpose. Teachers who exhibit vitality are energized by their own curiosities, their colleagues, and their students; they find joy and stimulation in the daily dilemmas of teaching and are intrigued by the challenge of improving adult learning communities. Teachers become fully alive when their schools and districts provide them with opportunities for skillful participation, inquiry, dialogue, and reflection. Such environments foster leadership.

It is no surprise that teacher leadership is at the heart of the high leadership capacity school. Because teachers represent the largest and most constant group of professionals in schools and districts, their full participation in the work of leadership is necessary for high leadership capacity. This is a comforting thought, because the path to leadership is so clear, yet also a

disquieting one, because many find the path difficult.

Why do so many principals and superintendents find teacher leadership so difficult to come by? There are several reasons: a philosophy that reserves the work of leadership for formal authority roles, a hierarchical view of authority and power, and an insistence that teachers could be coaxed into leadership if presented with the right incentives, to name a few. Such attitudes produce short-term, shallow, and unsustainable results. Using external incentives to motivate teachers, for instance, can have a deleterious effect on leadership. Short-term incentives that elicit mechanistic responses from some teachers can generate resentment in the long run by encouraging reliance on such rewards. True development is bound to be stunted by incentive systems unless they attend to intrinsic as well as extrinsic motivation, such as by offering increased opportunities to learn.

Recall the key assumptions about leadership in Chapter 1: that everyone has the right, responsibility, and capability to be a leader, and that it is in the adult learning environment that teacher leadership truly develops. Recall also that leading and learning are deeply intertwined, and that leading is fundamental to the nature and mission of teaching.

What Is a Teacher Leader?

Teacher leaders are those whose dreams of making a difference have either been kept alive or have been reawakened by engaging with colleagues and working within a professional culture.

Those for whom the dream has been kept alive are reflective, inquisitive, focused on improving their craft, and action-oriented; they accept responsibility for student learning and have a strong sense of self. They know their intentions well enough not to be intimidated into silence by others, are open to learning, and understand the three dimensions of learning in schools: student learning, the learning of colleagues, and learning of their own.

Teacher leaders might be reawakened to their sense of purpose by working within an improving school, or perhaps in a setting outside the school, such as through a network, a university program, or thoughtfully designed initiatives (the National Board Certification process, for example, or the National Writing Project). Those who rekindle their sense of purpose outside of the school may not be able to stay long inside it, especially if it isn't compatible with their renewed feelings about their mission as teachers. This is particularly true if the school has many Quadrant 1 or Quadrant 2 features—for instance, if it lacks a collegial culture, shared vision, or collective responsibility for student learning.

In the same way that everyone is born to learn, everyone is born to lead. The right-hand column of the Continuum of Teacher Leadership in Appendix C describes some common leadership characteristics. High leadership capacity schools provide teachers with opportunities for skillful participation, which in turn allows their leadership skills to flourish. The schools cited in Chapters 2 and 3 used participation and skillfulness to foster teacher leadership.

On Becoming a Teacher Leader

When thinking about teacher leadership, we should keep in mind the differences between actions and roles. Actions may precede or accompany roles; they may include asking thoughtful questions in a staff meeting, bringing a fresh perspective to a conversation, sharing ideas and practices with others, or initiating new ways of getting tasks accomplished. Though teachers may not always be in the position to take on new roles, they can always engage in acts of leadership.

Roles include sets of actions performed within a labeled framework. School council representative, team leader, department chair, teacher on special assignment, parent liaison, literacy coach—these are all common roles in schools and districts. Roles require us to tap new inner resources and adopt new responsibilities. In most roles, teachers need to understand and represent others, convene and lead conversations, identify and mobilize resources, and connect the thinking and planning of a given group with that of the whole staff. Such roles lead to a broader definition of what it means to be a teacher.

Here are three examples of particularly promising teacher leader roles that I've recently come across:

- Schools in Kansas City, Kansas, employ a School Improvement Facilitator (SIF) to serve one or two schools as a change agent to facilitate the learning conversations in the school. The SIF is chosen from outstanding teacher leaders, is highly trained, and participates in networks with similar leaders on an ongoing basis.
- The intervention resource teacher in Cupertino, California, offers support for at-risk children and functions as a whole-school change agent by helping to develop curriculum, providing in-service training, coaching and mentoring new teachers, and serving as a liaison to initiatives outside the school. This role falls somewhere between teacher and administrator, and draws from the best of both worlds.
- The assistant principal in Calgary, Canada, is not only responsible for many management duties but also serves as a schoolwide change agent, like the SIF and the Intervention Resource Teacher. Careful attention is given to selection, nurturing, and performance of the assistant principals in Calgary, including a major annual conference and systematic professional development. (Assistant principals are teacher leaders in Alberta, as school administrators are part of the teaching force.)

Leadership Actions

Many actions are essential to teacher leadership, but I will give special attention here to conversations related to coaching, learning communities, mentoring, and networking. To foster teacher leadership, we begin by initiating conversations. These come in many forms, including

- **One-on-one,** in which coaching questions are asked and ideas are shared;
- **Inquiring,** which revolves around dialogues about data;

- **Partnering,** in which educators engage with parents and community members; and
- **Sustaining,** during which long-range plans are developed.

All of these conversations share the following common elements (provided, of course, that they are undertaken with positive intent):

- Shared purpose
- Search for understanding
- Reflection on beliefs and experiences
- Revelation of ideas and information
- Respectful listening (Lambert et al., 1995, 2002)

As we have seen in Chapter 2, dialogues are the best types of conversations for evoking thoughts and feelings about our students and ourselves. Being listened to carefully and listening carefully to others has an almost magical effect on what we say: issues and problems are held at arms length and examined from all sides, instead of being subjected to quick opinions and ready solutions.

COACHING

Coaching stems from the same principles as dialogue, but entails an even more personal approach, since it usually occurs one on one. Although instructional coaching has been with us for many decades, very little attention has been given to *leadership* coaching, in which questions are meant to expand the respondent's focus from being a reflective practitioner to being a leader. This is reflected in the Continuum of Emerging Teacher Leadership in Appendix C, when respondents evolve from exhibiting the characteristics in the left-hand column to also exhibiting those in the right-hand column. In Figure 4.1, selected actions from the four categories of the continuum—adult development, dialogue, collaboration, and organizational

FIGURE 4.1

Examples of Leadership Coaching

Leadership Category	Reflective Practitioner Characteristics	Teacher Leader Characteristics	Coaching Questions
Adult Development	Understands self as interdependent with others in the school community; is contemplative and seeks feedback from others.	Helps colleagues to express their confidence and shared values and to form interdependent learning communities.	How might you share your leading perspective with others? What question would you ask your team members to discover the groups' shared values?
Dialogue	Communicates well with individuals and groups in the community to create and sustain relationships and focus on teaching and learning.	Facilitates effective dialogue among members of the school community in order to build relationships and focus the dialogue on teaching and learning.	What dialogue facilitation skills will you need to work with your team? What dialogue question would focus the team on teaching and learning?
Collaboration	Participates actively in shared decision making; volunteers to follow through on group decisions.	Promotes collaborative decision making to meet the diverse individual and group needs of the school community.	How might you encourage particular members of the school community to serve on the team? How effective is our current decision-making structure for our community?
Organizational Change	Develops forward-thinking skills for working with others and planning for school improvement. Bases future goals on shared values and vision.	Provides for and creates opportunities to engage others in visionary thinking and planning based on shared core values.	What process might help us translate our shared values into a school vision? How might we improve our planning for school improvement?

change—are matched with accompanying coaching questions.

As these examples suggest, coaching is an invaluable aspect of leadership development. And because student learning and adult learning are parallel ideas, leadership coaching can be linked with instructional coaching quite easily. Many of the same questions can be asked in both cases, including, "What is your desired outcome for your students/team?" "What role will you play in helping to achieve your objectives?" "What evidence will you look for to assess whether your student/team goals have been reached?"

LEADERSHIP MENTORING

Leadership mentors are usually teacher leaders themselves. In Chapter 3, we saw how the mentoring relationship between Principal Trevor and Jennifer led to her development as a teacher leader. This mentoring process involved coaching, feedback, modeling, provisions for leadership experiences, training, and participation in arenas outside of the classroom and school. Mentors often see greater possibility in their mentees than do the mentees themselves, who tend to live up to their mentors' expectations when a deep belief in their capacities is expressed. The mentoring process can help educators to become better at problem solving and decision making, offers both support and challenge, and facilitates a professional vision (Lipton & Wellman, 2001).

TEACHER LEADERSHIP SELF-ASSESSMENT

The Rubric of Emerging Teacher Leadership in Appendix B and the Continuum of Emerging Teacher Leadership in Appendix C can help educators assess their own leadership actions by helping them identify the skills and understandings critical to teacher leadership, as well as by serving as a supporting framework for conversations related to coaching, mentoring, and professional development.

High Leadership Capacity Schools As Learning Communities

The activities and relationships discussed above exist within a learning community: an environment that is vibrant and unified around the shared purpose of student learning. High leadership capacity schools are excellent learning communities, as both environments involve most of the same features, including shared vision, inquiry, reflective practice, and collective responsibility. The members of learning communities are bonded to a whole that is larger and stronger than the sum of its parts. In Chapters 2 and 3 we saw how schools enabled teachers to share ideas and knowledge that led to ways of creating shared knowledge together. A high leadership capacity school is one in which teachers choose to lead because their environment has allowed them to do so.

NETWORKS

Networks provide teachers with an extended learning community in which to develop their professional self-concepts. In regional or national networks, teachers see themselves as part of a broader profession and are listened to with an intensity and respect that may not exist in their schools; hearing and seeing how other teachers think and interact allow them to fine-tune their perceptions of their own roles as teachers. The National Writing Project is an excellent example of such a network. According to Lieberman and Wood (2001), its practices include:

- Approaching every colleague as a valued contributor
- Viewing teachers as experts
- Creating forums for sharing, dialogue, and critique
- Turning ownership of learning over to the learners

- Situating learning in practice and relationships, providing multiple entry points into learning communities, and adopting an inquiry stance
- Sharing leadership
- Rethinking professional identities and linking them to a professional community

Teachers in the project meet frequently to consider their difficulties reaching students and to share ideas and experiences. The National Writing Project flourishes best when participants are offered opportunities to learn, work as a community, and take on leadership responsibilities at the local site.

The many different approaches to teacher leadership support described in this book—conversation, collaboration, study groups, networks, etc.—can be provided by principals, colleagues, district personnel responsible for instruction, and school coaches. Figure 4.2 suggests strategies that principals or others might use for this purpose, along with the behavioral shifts expected of teachers in response to each strategy.

FIGURE 4.2
Building Leadership Capacity Through Commitment: A Few Benchmarks and Strategies

Benchmarks in the Development of Teacher Leadership	Principal Strategies That Encourage Teacher Leadership
Initiate new actions by suggesting other ways to accomplish tasks or goals	**Create** opportunities for dialogue that deepens understanding of issues
Solve problems instead of asking permission and assigning blame	**Shift** from a permission-giving or withholding stance to one of consistent problem solving (whether one-on-one or in small or large groups)
Volunteer to take responsibility for issues or tasks	**Surface** issues and conditions without knowing the answer; raise questions without easy answers
Invite other teachers to work with them, share materials, and visit classrooms	**Continually indicate** that time is available for shared work—offer to cover classrooms, ask staff to attend professional development activities in pairs, and build small-group conversations into every faculty meeting
Listen to each other, and particularly to new members of the staff	**Model** respectful listening in every setting; do not rush communications
Admit to mistakes and unsolved instructional issues and ask for assistance from colleagues	Do the same
Talk about children in a way that suggests that all children can learn	**Model** the same behavior, ask probing questions (including ones without easy answers), use reflective strategies in faculty meetings, and invite a high level of risk taking
Become more skillful in conversations, facilitation, asking inquiry questions, and teaching	**Become more skillful** at facilitating conversations, reflection, and designing faculty interaction time

Enculturation of New Teachers and Principals

Enculturation can imply a process of training educators to assume traditional roles that protect the status quo. You know the rhetoric: "Don't speak up for the first three years," "Don't sit in that chair," "Don't ask questions," "Our last principal didn't ask us to do *his* work!" "Our motto is 'sink or swim.'" But enculturation can also mean helping new teachers and principals to hit the road running, welcoming them to the staff from the very beginning, and encouraging them to become part of a strong learning community. This second definition is the one I wish to focus on here.

NEW AND BEGINNING TEACHERS

Thoughtful enculturation is critical to sustainability and can help weave the cloth of community together so that sharp shifts in the school culture—the arrival of many new teachers, for example—do not disrupt the flow of the school's improvement processes.

Janet Gless, associate director of the New Teacher Center at the University of California, Santa Cruz, points out that support for beginning teachers can contribute to building leadership capacity. Veteran teachers benefit by assuming the important professional leadership role of mentor, thus accepting responsibility for the professional success of their colleagues (much as they do, in their roles as classroom teachers, for the success of their students). Veteran teachers powerfully influence their new colleagues by modeling the professional norms and behaviors that contribute to quality instruction and teacher leadership, such as engaging in reflective inquiry about classroom practice, focusing on and accepting responsibility for student learning, striving continuously to learn new skills and adapt them to classroom practice, and

valuing colleagueship and professional dialogue in the service of high professional standards.

In Saratoga, California, new-teacher mentors are known as "buddy teachers" and help newcomers with such tasks as preparing the learning environment, getting ready for their first open house and parent conferences, securing materials and resources (including discretionary funds for purchasing materials), orienting themselves to programs and texts, and generally negotiating the many logistical and management duties of teaching. All teachers in Saratoga serve as buddy teachers, and thus remain familiar with the challenges facing new teachers. This awareness enables the voices of novices to be heard and acknowledged. In addition to buddy teachers, all new teachers are assigned "consulting teachers" to observe their teaching, coach them, and engage them in professional planning and self-assessment. By learning the principles of adult learning and successful practice, developing coaching skills, and creating learning experiences for their colleagues, new-teacher mentors, buddies, and consultants develop important leadership skills of their own.

Teacher induction programs that provide adequate sanctioned time for new teachers to work with their mentor colleagues can help develop leaders from the very beginning. Induction programs teach new recruits to communicate their dilemmas, discoveries, and accomplishments to other colleagues, and allow new teachers to begin their careers understanding the value of an environment that supports adult learning and, by extension, teacher leadership. Effective induction programs help new teachers to focus on their capacity to make a difference in the learning of individual students, thus helping keep their passion for teaching alive. Guided by professional standards and the understanding that teacher learning is essential for successful practice, new teachers can emerge as leaders early in their careers.

In California, professional standards for teachers emerged out of the work of new-teacher induction. Adopted statewide in 1997, the California Standards for the Teacher Profession (CSTP) provide a vision of what accomplished teaching can be. The six standards are:

- Engaging and supporting all students in learning
- Creating and maintaining effective environments for student learning
- Understanding and organizing subject matter for student learning
- Planning instruction and designing learning experiences for all students
- Assessing student learning
- Developing as a professional educator

It is important to have a way to describe the discrete steps in a teacher's journey toward leadership, and the New Teacher Center at the University of California, Santa Cruz, has developed a continuum of teacher practice aligned with the CSTP. The sixth dimension of this continuum, "developing as a professional educator," highlights the following six leadership skills and dispositions:

- Collegial dialogue
- Professional contributions
- Innovation
- Communication
- Collaboration
- Professional integrity

As a whole, the continuum helps new teachers assess their practice and set the next steps necessary for professional growth. The assessment is collaborative and uses artifacts of classroom practice, such as rubrics developed in the classroom, as evidence of the teacher's developmental level. Not only does this help the new teacher become articulate about her practice,

but it also teaches her to provide evidence demonstrating her level of accomplishment and to understand that the improvement of practice is a career-long journey best made in the company of colleagues.

New and Beginning Principals

Enculturation of principals is not nearly as common as enculturation of teachers. Even the best of teachers might stand back and wait for the principal to fail or figure things out for himself. In a school interested in sustainability and high leadership capacity, this kind of stance is highly unproductive.

I suggest that teachers realize that they play a large role in ensuring the success of a new principal. Naturally, I recognize that districts sometimes act unilaterally and irresponsibly by placing autocratic principals in schools that had been moving toward higher leadership capacity, and such actions are difficult to defend. But in most cases, teachers can help the principal by meeting with him to explain the school culture and its successful programs, alert him to concerns, offer assistance, and coach him. Because the new principal will have much to offer as well, such a meeting is a chance to establish reciprocal relationships and establish that professionals have many things to learn from each other. Approached in this way, relationships with principals can be constructed in healthy and productive ways right from the beginning.

Barriers to Teacher Leadership

Barriers to teacher leadership abound: lack of time, misconceptions of equity (e.g., "no teacher is different than another"), hierarchical cultures of authority, peer opposition, and a desire for harmony and safety over conflict and risk are just a few of the factors that discourage teachers from leading. The higher the leadership capacity of a school, the more these constraining factors seem to dissolve into the background. But in a Quadrant 1 school, these barriers dominate, allowing educators to blame external forces and avoid responsibility. It is not uncommon to hear the following types of comments in a Quadrant 1 school:

- "If the 6th grade teacher had taught my 7th graders to be responsible for their homework, we wouldn't have these problems."
- "I'm not paid to do administrative work; let the principal make the decision."
- "Joe left in his third year. He didn't understand what it meant to teach here. He was always volunteering to work with the principal and that doesn't bode well at our school."
- "I teach the students who are ready to learn."

By the time a school nears Quadrant 4 status, those who had previously built barriers will now be participating, or at least not undermining the efforts of those who are. Having gained experience with leading, support, and feedback, Quadrant 4 educators can help cultivate leadership among colleagues. As teachers become more skillful in their work with one another, their confidence grows, they come to see themselves differently, and the boundaries of teaching broaden to include the classroom, the school, the community, and the profession.

Teachers who have been in their positions for at least three years will have developed some routines, both in the classroom and in the rest of their professional lives, that must be "unlearned" if they are to become true leaders. Of course, we see from our students' experiences that unlearning long-held habits is often difficult. A constructivist approach to leadership is therefore particularly important. We begin the journey away from old habits of mind by examining

current assumptions, beliefs, and experiences: How do I now think of teacher leadership? What assumptions do I hold? What experiences have I had? Teachers who are unwilling to do this are often thought of as resistant.

Intervening with "Resistant" Teachers

Unfortunately, some teachers have been disappointed once too often by unfulfilled promises, or have drawn tight boundaries around their professional lives, and are consequently resistant to change. Even if there are only a few such teachers in a school, they can draw energy from the whole and may even sabotage the community's work in an effort to sustain the status quo. Resistant teachers often refuse to participate in productive ways, envision themselves as learners, contribute to the learning of other adults, or observe norms of civil and professional behavior.

The school environment is the most significant contributor to resistance: teachers who resist building leadership capacity in schools with Quadrant 1 norms will perform differently in Quadrant 4 schools. Each environment brings out different inner resources and attitudes from individuals, creating the theater in which behaviors are learned and practiced.

In a Quadrant 4 school, teachers tend either to develop the relationships suggested in Figure 4.2 or leave the school (either by transferring, changing professions, or retiring). The relationships suggest an interdependent learning community in which teachers take collective responsibility for the school. When encouraging teachers to improve their practice, it is essential to provide them with support from administrators and colleagues in the form of clear expectations, classroom observations and instructional coaching, professional development, rich opportunities for satisfaction with intrinsic rewards, supervision, and evaluation. Working with a teacher who is resisting the process of professional learning can be tiring, but if the resistant teacher is harmful to student learning and development, the energy to either improve or remove the teacher is well spent. As a rule, educators should spend the most energy on teachers who *want* to participate in skillful ways.

Sustaining Teacher Leadership Over Time

We sustain teacher leadership by establishing and maintaining high leadership capacity and supporting and developing leadership among new teachers. Leadership capacity involves an infrastructure for learning composed of roles and responsibilities, inquiry, reflection, and a focus on student learning. The professional staff must be continually replenished by new faculty who hit the road running thanks to the school's provisions for orientation, new knowledge, support, and mentoring.

Still, some teacher leaders do burn out. Sustained, high-quality performance can be exhausting. When I worked as a principal, I had a teacher named Kit who woke up one day and decided her plate was too full: in addition to her school responsibilities, she was the mother of two young sons. She decided she would take the semester off—not from teaching, but from leading in special roles. Her colleagues and I agreed that she needed to step back and refresh herself. The next fall she returned to her new roles at the school revitalized.

I learned a lot from Kit. Dropping back doesn't mean dropping out. We need to calibrate our energies in order to hang in for the long haul. Sustainability requires us to think anew about dedication, time, and responsibilities. As we support each other in this journey toward leadership capacity, we need to keep in mind our total lives: who we are as professionals, parents, spouses, children, and community

members. All of us yearn for the vitality and purpose that make our lives meaningful. Much, but not all, of this purpose can be found in school.

Activities and Questions

1. Begin a group dialogue by asking: "What is teacher leadership, and what does it look like in our school?" Summarize ideas from the group on chart paper. Leave the charts up on the staff room wall for people to add ideas.

2. Read the following Roland Barth passage (1999) and discuss in teams:

> Teachers who choose the path of teacher leadership experience:
>
> - a reduction of isolation, which comes from frequent companionship and collegiality among other adults;
> - the personal and professional satisfaction that comes from improving their schools;
> - a sense of instrumentality, investment, and membership in the school community;
> - new learning about the schools, the process of change and about themselves, which accompanies being a leader;
> - and professional invigoration and replenishment, which spill over into their classroom teaching. These teachers become owners and investors in their schools, rather than mere tenants.

3. In small teams, explore the obstacles to teacher leadership in your school. Divide a piece of paper into four columns labeled "Self," "School," "District," and "Profession." Under each column, list the relevant factors that get in the way of teacher leadership. Share with your team members and with the larger group.

4. In a staff or team meeting, divide into small groups and read through the Rubric of Emerging Teacher Leadership (Appendix B). Assess each dimension by placing a mark on the

continuum line at the top of the rubric that best represents you. Select three areas of potential growth toward greater teacher leadership and discuss your plans. Suggest to team members how they might support you.

5. At a faculty meeting, divide into pairs and discuss the following question for five minutes: "What strengths do I bring to the role of leader?" After discussing, write for five minutes on the same question. In small groups, share the strengths that you have identified for yourself, paying close attention to any patterns within the group. Examine the Rubric of Emerging Teacher Leadership for the strengths your group has just discussed. Discuss what you have discovered and possible uses of the rubric.

6. In pairs, refer to the Roland Barth quote above. Using Figure 4.1 as a reference, develop three questions each that could enable you to move toward greater teacher leadership.

7. Set a time to meet with your partner from activity six above to coach each other in leadership. Use the questions that you have developed as well as any others that occur to you during the session. Probe for specificity (e.g., "Tell me more about what you are thinking," "What would that look like?" "Give me an example.").

8. Establish coaching sessions twice a month. Combine these sessions with peer instructional coaching. Debrief as a whole group in staff or team meetings.

9. Develop a personal plan for teacher leadership. Consider the following questions:

- What major understandings have you developed about yourself as you have experienced and read about teacher leadership?
- Visualize the teacher leader you would like to be. What does she do and say?
- How does she respond to others?
- What additional skills, knowledge, or attitudes will you need in order to achieve your desired image of a teacher leader? How will you develop these skills, knowledge, and attitudes?
- What do you want your students to say about you 20 years from now?

CHAPTER 5
The Changing Role of the Principal

Although teachers are at the heart of leadership capacity, principals hold a special position in schools. They have access to the larger school system, a claim to organizational and historical authority, and the pressure to meet teacher, parent, and student expectations. They build trust, focus the school, convene and sustain the conversation, and insist on the implementation of policy and practice. As long as we have schools that need to be improved or improvements that need to be sustained, the role of the principal will be important.

By following the chapter on teacher leadership with this chapter on principals, I hope to imply that the major undertaking of the principal is working with and through the adult community in the school. Because teachers, not principals, teach all the school's students, it is vital that the principal's interactions with

teachers enable the school to focus purposefully on student learning.

However, in some regions of the country, the role of the principal is undergoing a profound change. We now know that a principal who is collaborative, open, and inclusive can accomplish remarkable improvements in schools and deeply affect student learning. In this chapter, I will describe the many challenges principals face on the road to building leadership capacity. This is a lifelong journey, and will require a shift in perspective for many.

Shifting Principal Perspectives

Capacity-building principals align their actions to the belief that everyone has the right, responsibility, and capability to work as a leader. Such a perspective requires that principals be clear about their own core values and confident in their own capacity to work well with others by influencing, facilitating, guiding, and mentoring. They need to resist using authority to tell and command.

Sometimes I hear it said that no one style of leadership is any better than another. I'm afraid that this just isn't so: some styles *are* preferable to others. Goleman (1995) suggests that one of the critical elements of a healthy leadership perspective is emotional intelligence. The emotionally intelligent principal is self-motivating and empathic, persists toward the goal of educating all children, manages his emotions and stress so as not to lose sight of his core values and commitments, and perhaps most importantly, holds on tightly to hope. These individuals are able to create organizational climates of trust, information sharing, healthy risk-taking, and learning. In short, as Goleman points out, good guys finish first. The characeristics listed here validate the image of a Quadrant 4 principal: open, collaborative, and clear about what is important—student learning—and how to work with others to achieve it.

Principals confront the work of building leadership capacity from many different perspectives, most often from one of four approaches:

- **Directive:** engages in command-and-control behavior.
- **Laissez-faire:** makes the decisions behind the scenes without involving others systematically, creating organizational uncertainty and fragmentation.
- **Collaborative:** encourages open participation, but is unsure how to involve those who don't choose to be involved. May unwittingly prolong dependency behaviors and dispositions inherited from previous years.
- **Capacity-building:** creates meaning and shared knowledge through broad-based, skillful participation.

While the evolution of effective leadership is developmental, these types cannot be said to follow each other in linear fashion: the directive principal seldom becomes laissez faire, but the collaborative principal will often become capacity-building. If we were to think of a continuum, it might look something like this:

Directive ↘

       Collaborative → Capacity-building

Laissez faire ↗

The Directive Principal

The directive principal is a synthesis of prior experience, personality style, and a reinforcing top-down system. He does not lack for clarity—he is in charge and knows what needs to be done—but, unfortunately, seldom does the right thing. Directive or command-and-control behavior may get the immediate task done, but it undermines the growth and development of those who are subjected to it, diminishing teacher leadership and the leadership capacity of the school. Innovation, risk-taking, and real conversations about teaching and learning are not to be found in schools governed by directive principals (which is not to suggest that they do not occasionally need to make direct or unilateral decisions). When a directive principal is appointed to a school with a high leadership capacity, teachers will leave, close their doors and turn inward, become cynical, display dependency behaviors, or seek to have the principal dismissed.

The Laissez-Faire Principal

The laissez-faire principal is most often encountered in a large school. Though she may be quite competent in many ways, her leadership style creates a school that is fragmented and individualistic, and which lacks program coherence. There are two reasons for this. One is a lack of a shared purpose or vision to focus commitment, leading to practices, policies, and programs that are all over the place, often unrelated and disconnected. Instruction at a school with a laissez-faire principal may reflect teacher creativity, for example, but not common learning goals. As we saw in Chapter 1, one of the most negative implications of this practice is that vulnerable children fall through the cracks.

The other reason is that the laissez-faire principal makes decisions according to the situation at hand, without fitting it into a larger context; consequently, her decisions lack consistency and may even contradict each other. In addition, the laissez-faire principal rarely asks what groups or teams should be involved with a given decision, what process should be used to achieve her goals, or how her decisions connect with other practices and policies in the school.

The Collaborative Principal

Lori Abramson, director of education at Temple Sinai School in Oakland, California, is an example of an insightful collaborative principal who made the transition to a capacity-building principal. She described to me how she came to realize that she wasn't achieving the goals she'd originally set out for herself:

> When I read *Building Leadership Capacity in Schools,* it was as if I had been struck by lightning. For ten years as Director of Education in a religious education setting, I had strived to create the perfect conditions for teachers, students, and families. I aspired to a collegial and collaborative atmosphere for teachers, processes for feedback from everyone, openness to ideas, opportunities for reflection, and avenues for leadership development. What a shock to realize that what I had in fact created for my staff was a top-down, hier-

archical model of staff development and supervision! I set the agendas, I decided what teachers needed to study, and I functioned as a classic bottleneck! Obviously, these results were the antithesis of the kind of educational leader I desire to be.

Lori realized that the four-step process of reflection, dialogue, inquiry, and action was identical to the process she and her education committee had developed over the years of working together. (The Temple Sinai education committee is a group of volunteer parents who set vision and policy for the synagogue's educational programs.) Guided by the principles of building leadership capacity, Lori resolved to change the reality of staff development in their school. Here Lori describes some of the changes she and the committee instituted (personal communication, 2001):

- We arranged teachers in teams by grade-level with mentor teachers functioning as team leaders. The teams meet regularly to discuss successes and issues in their classrooms and support each other. The team leaders then meet with me to share the information and to ensure that everyone in need of any kind of support receives it.
- During the year, we set four extended meetings attended by all staff members to study larger issues together and design action plans.
- We reworked how we pay teachers for continuing education. In the past we provided onsite presentations about a particular topic during the above-mentioned extended meeting time. Now we offer a stipend to every teacher who completes eight hours of learning on his own time. (Courses need to be related to curriculum or pedagogy and school goals.)
- To introduce the process of building leadership capacity, we chose the issue of building community within our school. Engaging in

the four-step process with the staff, we have been able to see progress in all of the areas examined by the education committee over the past several years: quality of teaching; staff training; mentoring; school and program evaluation; discipline; family, student, and staff investment and involvement in Jewish education; and communication with families. The culture of our school has begun to change from one of dependency and bottlenecks to one of responsibility, teamwork, and efficacy. It has been a true joy as an educator to witness these changes.

Lori's journey is not unusual. Caring, nurturing, and ready to serve, she created a culture in which she was the pivotal individual—everything funneled through her. Yet Lori's personal capacity for reflection and wisdom led her in a new direction. She has become a capacity-building principal.

The Capacity-Building Principal

Joan Burr, principal of Angel Hills Adult School, told me about her own journey into capacity-building leadership. She sought to open communication and respect the voices of staff while enabling them to experience and appreciate several reflective processes:

> Sitting in a department staff meeting that was being conducted by one of the department coordinators, I found myself wrestling with my own emotions. I could not believe the behavior of some of the teachers as the coordinator attempted to facilitate a discussion. What appeared as a complete lack of respect for the coordinator and the topic made me very angry. As I controlled the temptation to ask, "What is going on here?" I convinced myself to step back to try to gain a better understanding of what brought this group of experienced teachers to this point.

It just so happened that *I was in the midst of a profound professional development experience of my own*, learning about building collaboration and shared leadership as part of my educational administration training. I decided to accept the challenge of addressing this severe and long-standing morale issue within the department. In order to understand how staff had or had not felt involved, I conducted an in-depth interview with each teacher and coordinator and convened three group meetings to share what I had discovered and for the group to identify means for improvement. The meetings included the creation of norms and small and large group dialogues. The process created a climate in which individuals were able to share the many slights and perceptions that have developed over the years.

One of the outcomes of this process was the identification and implementation of more effective systems for communication. A framework for a higher level of involvement by teachers in program decision-making was also identified. Each one of us increased our personal capacity for effective communication and participation in a collaborative team. Was I nervous? You bet! But I think the learning that occurred for all of us greatly contributed to the spirit of "We are in this together, let's find our way together!"

These four styles of principal leadership significantly affect the existing or potential leadership capacity of a school. It is our compelling task as educators to negotiate paths through rough terrain and the sometimes conflicting messages from those around us. Clarity about our own values and aspirations can serve as the beam of light in the occasional fog of our journey.

As you consider your own style of leading, pay particular attention to behaviors that result in a *controlling culture*. Ask yourself some of these questions:

- How was the last important decision made in our school? Did it involve those affected by the decision?
- When asked for a decision, do I make it without thinking about the process or including others?
- When I observe teachers, students, or staff members doing things that I consider unacceptable, do I quickly correct and redirect them or do I involve them in a problem-solving conversation about the behavior?
- Do I get overly frustrated with process and long for the day when I could just do it myself?
- Do I delegate tasks only to take them back if things aren't going the way I want them to go?

Paying attention to ourselves—a process known as metacognition—is an essential attribute of any effective learner or leader. At the end of this chapter, an activity will ask you to closely examine your own style and any plans for deepening its effective qualities, developing new dimensions, or abandoning some old behaviors.

Jennifer's Transition

It will not surprise you that Jennifer is now principal of Belvedere School. As a teacher in a Quadrant 4 school, she has had many advantages, and along the way has experienced, witnessed, and practiced excellent leading behaviors. Her colleagues welcomed her with open arms as their new principal. Though they celebrated Principal Trevor's tenure, they were able to forgo the grieving process that often accompanies the loss of a good principal thanks to Jennifer's ascension to the post.

Yet something had changed. Although she was determined to continue as a colleague, remnants of traditional positional authority, access to system information and offices, and her new

role as an evaluator marked a new day. How would she reconstruct relationships with respected peers? How would she redefine herself without losing her integrity as a leader?

Jennifer brought up the issue of her changing role with faculty and staff members and discussed what she thought the effect on school staff would be, as well as her apprehensions and her need to negotiate her own path. She shared that she was committed to the direction in which the school was moving—its philosophy, vision, and participation patterns. By beginning this conversation and returning it to the table as necessary, Jennifer and the rest of the Belvedere staff began to construct additional dimensions to the relationships that they had enjoyed for the past four years.

New Uses of Principal Authority

Jennifer knew that she had authority that she had not experienced as a teacher, and was determined to follow John Trevor's example and not rein in the authority that had been distributed to teachers, students, and parents. She was surprised that teachers were willing to give some of the authority back and see how she would handle it.

Authority derived from the state or province and embedded in formal leadership positions is a vital dimension of being a principal. Although once used in school to enable command-and-control behaviors, this is no longer desirable or productive. Instead, principals can use authority to facilitate the leadership capacity building process. Specifically, they need to

- Develop a shared vision based on community values;
- Organize, focus, and sustain the conversations about teaching and learning;
- Insist that student learning is at the center of the conversation;

- Protect and interpret community values, assuring a focus on and congruence with teaching and learning approaches;
- Work through the evaluation and district personnel systems to dismiss ineffective teachers (assuming that all other support systems have been used and did not succeed);
- Work with all participants to implement community decisions; and
- Develop reciprocal relationships with the larger system, such as by securing support and resources.

These are some of the major aspects of leadership authority. More managerial ones include legal authority regarding student or employee discipline, accounting supervision (rather than setting resource priorities unilaterally), building oversight, and teacher evaluation.

Breaking Dependencies

One of the traditional uses of authority has been to reinforce dependency behaviors among school staff. When a staff member asks permission from a directive principal, it may signal to the latter that he is definitely in control of the school. Asking permission from principals is a red flag, indicating that dependency relationships are getting in the way of building leadership capacity.

Dependency relationships are most often observed in a Quadrant 1 school, although some may linger as the school develops its leadership capacity as well. In Chapter 1, I noted that realigning relationships from dependency to reciprocity is often the major challenge of the Quadrant 1 school. Unless adult-to-adult relationships develop, true collegiality is almost impossible.

Two particular models of dependency tend to develop in organizations. One is a *hierarchical*

dependency on the principal to make the major decisions, give or withhold information and permission, and direct the work of the school. The other, *codependency,* is harder to overcome: both the principal and the teachers depend on each other to keep old patterns of behavior in place. The principal signals verbally and nonverbally that the teacher is to remain in an old role, such as attending to the classroom and not getting involved in the business of the school, and the teacher signals to the principal that top-down management is desired.

As Barbara Kohm, former principal at Captain School in Clayton, Missouri, told me:

> When I first became a principal, teachers brought many problems to me which I worked hard to help them solve in a thoughtful and intelligent way. Unfortunately, however, *the more adept I became at solving problems, the weaker the school became.* We were constantly reacting to difficult situations rather than planning to prevent them, and our solutions were limited by my understanding and experience. Every problem I solved created three or four new ones. We needed a planning process that prevented problems from occurring and engaged the thinking and experience of every faculty member. By pooling our experiences we made better decisions and learned from one another.

When a principal—rather than the school community members—consistently solves problems, makes decisions, and gives answers, dependency behaviors on the part of staff actually increase. Yet, there are some "protections" that principals can offer that actually provide staff members with more freedom to act. Conzemius (1999) points out that when teachers are incubating new ideas and programs, they should be protected from myths and rumors, outside pressures, administrative burdens, and even early visitation requests in order to hold the world at bay while new ideas are being born.

It is important to monitor your behaviors as a principal and keep in mind the danger of dependency. Figure 5.1 describes strategies for breaking dependency relationships and realigning relationships. (See Appendix G for an essay by an elementary school principal on how to foster leadership capacity in others.)

The Principal As Learner and Developer of Leadership Capacity

Throughout this book, I have suggested a deep connection between learning and leading. This understanding is particularly vital for the principal as learner for it is such a leader who can model learning for others, presuppose that questions are open for exploration, and be

FIGURE 5.1
Strategies to Help Principals Break Dependency Relationships

- When asked permission for an action, do not say "yes" or "no." Shift the conversation to a problem-solving set of interactions with questions such as: "Tell me about what you have in mind." "What results do you anticipate?" "What resources are needed?" and "How can I be supportive?"
- Seek advice across role groups. For example, ask new teachers and members of the custodial staff for advice; seek out senior teachers as consultants or historians; convene groups of parents for consulting conversations. Encourage a genuine exchange of ideas.
- Redirect a permission-seeking conversation by asking if the individual would take responsibility for thinking the issue through: "I'll give you my ideas, but it would be helpful to have the ideas of others as well. Whom might you talk to?"
- Establish options or choices by brainstorming with individuals or groups; encourage choice among viable options.
- Use language that suggests community rather than ownership: Instead of "my budget," "my staff," or "my school," say, "*our* budget," "*our* staff," and "*our* school."
- When asked for a quick decision when one isn't required (e.g., the school isn't on fire), consider who or what groups need to be involved. Are you the best person to make this decision? What will the consequences be if you do make it?
- Rotate the leadership of faculty and team meetings, parent gatherings, and student assemblies.
- Clarify decision rules with the staff ahead of time. Include rules about which decisions are consulting or consensus decisions, which are for the faculty to make, which are for the principal to make alone, and which are made elsewhere.
- Get out from behind your desk; minimize symbols of authority.
- Let it be known that you don't have all the answers, but that you expect to work together to discover them.
- Do what you say you will do. Uncertainty and lack of dependability undermine trust and contribute to a culture of dependency.

increasingly effective in the work of building leadership capacity. Excitement for learning generates energy, and an expectation for learning becomes the norm.

Principal Jeff Pechura of Jefferson Elementary School in Wauwatosa, Wisconsin, refers to himself as "head learner." In his 2002 research study, "What Principals Do to Build and Sustain the Leadership Capacity of Teachers, Parents, and Students in Elementary Schools" (see Appendix G), Pechura examined principal behaviors in three high leadership capacity schools. His revealing insights into the work of the principal as he builds and sustains leadership capacity are consistent with the actions of other principals whose work informs this book. Figure 5.2 describes attributes that are particularly important for principals who are developing leadership capacity, and Figure 5.3 lists fifteen action steps to help them achieve this goal.

The following skills, understandings, and dispositions enable principals to help develop leadership capacity in their schools. The principal must:

1. Know himself and clarify his values. Such understanding becomes the mental model from which congruent behaviors and decisions can emerge, and the foundation for all actions. Several university preparation programs exist with this aim in mind.

2. Extend these understandings to the school and staff. Knowledge of the history and strengths and needs of the school, as well as of the leadership qualities of its staff.

3. Formally and informally assess the leadership capacity of the school. (See Chapter 3.)

4. Vow to work from the school's present state and walk side-by-side with staff toward further improvement, rather than impose a prepackaged agenda on the school.

5. Build trust. This is a result of honesty, respect, and follow-through.

6. Develop norms (see Chapter 2). This task is crucial, and can be achieved by establishing the professional boundaries of mutual respect and working agreements.

7. Establish mutual understanding with staff about decision rules that clarify which decisions are made through consultation, advisement, consensus, individual choice, or not at all. The principal reserves the responsibility to make certain personnel, legal, and emergency decisions.

8. Develop a shared vision. The vision is the touchstone for all other actions—the yardstick for questions and the reference point for conversations. If such a vision already exists, convene a conversation in order to make sense of it. Staff members should ask themselves what children and adults are doing that tells us our vision is alive and well. (For a discussion of the relationship between school and district visions, see Chapter 9.)

9. Develop leadership capacity in others. Such development is central to our journey. As leadership is developed, participants will develop their own theories of leadership. What is it? How do I see myself as a leader? What actions on my part evoke leadership from others? The development of such theories can be made explicit by a principal who makes leadership part of the conversation, study, observation, and feedback processes in faculty meetings, study groups, and leadership coaching sessions (Ackerman, Donaldson, & Van Der Bogert, 1996).

10. Establish the leadership team as a design team. A major task of the leadership team is to design the conversations. This includes the design of faculty meetings, study groups, teams, and other patterns of participation. (For guidance on the role, selection, and procedures for such a team, see Figure 2.1.)

FIGURE 5.2

Essential Principal Behaviors for Building Leadership Capacity

- **Clarify** their own values and engage others in forming and adhering to a shared vision of schooling
- **Design** and implement multiple participation patterns and groups (e.g., study groups, leadership teams, action research teams, parent councils, and student focus groups)
- **Facilitate** conversations and dialogue leading to shared purpose and actions
- **Provide** opportunities for others to learn and practice leadership skills
- **Invite** others into leadership roles and actions
- **Engage** educators, parents and community members, and students in a "cycle of learning" that involves reflection, dialogue, inquiry, construction of meaning, decision making, and action
- **Pose** questions that focus attention on what is most important (i.e., the school vision)
- **Develop, share,** and **invite** open information. Create information systems that cycle throughout the school community
- **Facilitate** communication among participants about the shared vision of the school; continually create, reinterpret, and deepen indicators of progress toward that vision
- **Seek** to broaden and reinforce roles that involve multiple levels of responsibility: to the classroom, the school community, the profession, and society
- **Create** and **facilitate** reciprocal learning
- **Promote** collective responsibility; involve others in determining criteria for success and taking responsibility for progress or lack thereof
- **Encourage** individual and group initiative by providing school community members with multiple resources (e.g., time, money, personnel, access to outside networks)
- **Facilitate** the development of internal accountability criteria and structures
- **Work** with the school community and district to establish standards and benchmarks that challenge all students
- **Design** (with others) professional development opportunities directed toward state-of-the-art instruction, assessment, and guidance for students
- **Establish** assessment programs that involve formative and summative student and parent reflection on products and performance
- **Ensure** that guidance programs address the resiliency needs of students: the presence of caring adults, problem-solving and goal-setting skills, access to a social network, opportunities for participation and contribution, and high expectations of achievement

11. Convene and sustain the conversations about teaching, learning, and leading. These conversations are well designed, facilitated, sequenced, and articulated. In other words, these are opportunities to construct meaning and theories of practice through regular dialogue, reflection, and inquiry. This is not to suggest that the principal is necessarily the

FIGURE 5.3

15 Leadership Capacity Action Steps for Principals

1. Know yourself—clarify your values
2. Extend your understandings to school and staff
3. Assess the leadership capacity of your school
4. Vow to work from the school's current condition and walk side-by-side with other staff
5. Build trust through honesty, respect, and follow-through
6. Develop community norms
7. Establish decision-making rules
8. Create a shared vision
9. Develop leadership capacity in others, including theories about leadership
10. Establish a leadership team as a design team
11. Convene and sustain regular in-depth conversations
12. Establish a cycle of inquiry
13. Develop goals and plans for action
14. Engage in communication processes designed to develop trust, relationships, and leadership; provoke quality performance; and implement community decisions
15. Develop a reciprocal relationship with district personnel

chief or lone facilitator, only that he makes sure the conversations continue.

12. Establish a cycle of inquiry. As we have seen, a cycle of inquiry is a way of continuing conversations based on questions, evidence, reflection, and action.

13. Create goals and plans of action for student learning as a result of the inquiry process, which also establishes an internal accountability system that enables staff members to continually monitor and evaluate their own actions.

14. Hone communication processes by questioning, coaching, breaking dependencies, being open, confronting conflict, and challenging norms. These processes are designed to develop trust, relationships, and leadership; provoke quality performance; implement community decisions; and ensure student learning.

15. Develop a reciprocal relationship with district personnel. By "reciprocal relationship," I mean that influence, in the form of both support and pressure, is mutual. (For details on the role of the district in building leadership capacity, see Chapter 9.)

These fifteen actions form an outline for the principal as she builds leadership capacity. Each action includes numerous other behaviors as well, many of which will occur repeatedly. The leadership capacity journey is continuous and doesn't stop at any destination. We can be inspired by the hope that, unlike many others, this journey is sustainable.

Conclusion

Principal leadership is key to the development of leadership capacity. But leadership in the service of what? Thus far, I have discussed leadership in terms of the development of the school's adult community. In Chapter 6 I will focus on the first major goal of leadership capacity: developing the learning and leadership of students.

Activities and Questions

1. Ask the following questions in a journal: How do I now see myself as a leader? What assumptions do I hold? Are my actions aligned with my beliefs? Revisit this journal regularly as a way to monitor your own development and keep yourself on course.

2. Do you see yourself as a directive, laissez-faire, collaborative, or capacity-building leader? Or are you some combination of these? Why do you see yourself this way? Explain to a trusted colleague.

3. Interview three staff members about how they observe your use of formal authority. Compare your responses. Are you perceived the same way by all? Why or why not?

4. Identify a person on staff with whom you may have a dependency relationship. Using some of the strategies in Figure 5.1, set about to realign that association into a more reciprocal relationship. Set a timeline for yourself. Write the results in a journal and share with a colleague.

5. Study Figure 5.2. Place a plus (+) sign beside behaviors that you are performing well and a question mark (?) beside those you wish to further explore. Discuss with your immediate supervisor or mentor as part of a personal professional development plan.

CHAPTER 6
Student Learning and Leading

In discussing high leadership capacity at Belvedere school, Jennifer described the many successes the school had seen in student learning: scores on state administered tests rose every year, writing samples revealed creative and technical improvements and a strong sense of student voice, public exhibitions displayed high-quality products and performances, and focus group data told of substantial opportunities for participation and leadership. Jennifer noted that such successes were the main reason for building leadership capacity.

Leadership has been defined as "reciprocal, purposeful learning in community." As we have already seen, learning and leading are firmly linked: a school with high leadership capacity develops students who both learn and lead. The schools described in this book enjoy high or steadily improving student performance and

development, regardless of ethnic makeup or socioeconomic levels. This is not surprising: schools in which staff members discuss student learning outcomes during continuing professional dialogues tend to reflect upon and improve practice as a result.

Students develop and learn in environments where adults do the same. There are at least three reasons for this. When adults have opportunities to skillfully participate in leadership, their perspectives about the world around them—including judgments as to who can learn and who can lead—expand; they achieve higher levels of moral development and can successfully grapple with challenging issues, such as equity; and they extend to others the opportunity to encounter similar experiences and learning. Adult leaders who build the leadership capacity of their schools create learning environments and experiences for students that result in

- Academic achievement as gauged by both authentic performance measures and test scores;
- Positive involvement: good attendance, few suspensions, low dropout rate, high graduation rate, and parent and student satisfaction;
- Resiliency behaviors such as self-direction, problem solving, social competence, participation, contributions to others, and a sense of purpose and future;
- Equitable gains across socioeconomic, race, ethnicity, and gender groups;
- A closing of the "achievement gap"; and
- Sustained improvements over time.

Student achievement can now be directly and unmistakably traced to the presence or lack of conditions that create high leadership capacity in schools, including teaching and instructional excellence. This is equally true in schools where achievement gaps are the most confounding. Throughout the United States, for instance, only 12 percent of Latinos and 14 percent of blacks entering kindergarten leave high school prepared for a four-year college; gaps in reading and writing between ethnic racial groups have been increasing over the last ten years; and schools with more minority students have fewer computers and more outdated textbooks (Olsen, 2000).

Yet, there is also a heartening realization that these gaps need not exist. Schools that have established the features of high leadership capacity are making equitable gains across socioeconomic, ethnic, and gender groups. As Haycock observes, "What's most important is building the capacity of the instructional staff to bring kids up to those new standards" (2000). Conzemius and O'Neill (2001) insist that where there is shared responsibility for

student learning, every ethnic subgroup improves in academic performance: the objective is not necessarily high test scores but rather *the continuous improvement of student learning.* Rising test scores are simply one measure of achievement.

90/90/90 schools—in which more than 90 percent of the students are ethnic minorities, are eligible for free and reduced lunch, and meet high academic standards—are a striking example of the possibility of success with all students. Reeves (2000) points out that 90/90/90 schools focus clearly on student achievement, assess student progress frequently through external scoring, provide multiple opportunities to improve achievement, and emphasize writing skills. Reeves contends that these improvements occur when teachers are involved in improving practice together within a professional culture. According to Lewis (2002), "In Chicago, wherever teachers had created strong professional communities with frequent teacher collaboration, reflective dialogue, and shared norms schools were four times more likely to be improving academically than schools with weaker professional communities."

How do students emerge as learners and leaders? The same approaches to fostering student leadership advance student learning, because leading is a *form* of learning. Educators can make the following key assumptions about student leadership:

- All children have the right, responsibility, and capability to be leaders
- Leadership can be understood as reciprocal, purposeful learning in community
- Learning is deeply intertwined with leading
- Learning communities should be designed to evoke leadership from all children
- Leading is a public expression of learning; because every student can learn, every student can lead

- Our historical mission of developing an educated citizenry capable of improving a democratic society is a function of early student learning and leadership

These assumptions frame the discussion of student leadership in this book, challenge our beliefs about who can lead, and allow us to entertain a different world of learning for students that emphasizes democratic participation.

Student Voice and the Generation of Leadership

A student leader is one who has found her own voice, contributes to the world around her, and understands that her future is integral to the success of her community and society. Student leadership emerges from democratic classrooms and schools in which student voices are invited and heard. Let's visit a few such classrooms here.

John and his 8th grade peers at Belvedere Middle School participate in a two-hour social science/language arts block at Belvedere. A strong sense of community pervades the room; the students know each other well, and together they create their own norms and are accountable for each other's learning. Skillful teams are involved in long-range projects of their choosing, each involving research online and in the community. The teams meet two mornings a week to share findings and learn new team, research, and writing skills, as well as to solve any problems they may be encountering. The teacher, Ms. Todd, facilitates, coaches, guides, and often participates in new learning. Ms. Todd, a social science/language arts core teacher who is also a member of a team, coordinates field research, projects, and final products with the science/math core. The same dedication to exploration, choice, and community can be found in the school as a whole.

Several principles of learning permeate Belvedere. It is understood, for instance, that student voice—the opportunity for students to express their ideas and beliefs and to be heard—leads to thoughtful choices in and out of the classroom, as well as to the growth of identity essential to student development. There are many opportunities for student voices to be heard at Belvedere, including involvement in action research, peer mediation and teaching, and school governance.

For years, Glenlawn Collegiate High School in Winnipeg, Canada, operated on the belief that the vast majority of its graduates went on to college, when in reality only about a third of them actually did so. Confronting old myths was an important part of the school's commitment to take a fresh look at its practice. In a collaborative exercise, teachers, students, parents, and community members undertook a research study of the post–high school choices of Glenlawn students. After analyzing the results of the study, this "college prep" school reoriented its curriculum toward three key skills: team building, problem solving, and lifelong learning. Students report that relationships developed through advisory and the use of portfolios to reflect on their work have enabled them to take responsibility for their own learning (Lambert & Gardner, 2002). Students today are choosing Glenlawn over other schools in a competitive market because it is known as a place where students report they are respected and purposeful. Enrollment is up and absenteeism is down; indeed, the school's success is often called "The Glenlawn Advantage."

At Richmond High School in California's West Contra Costa School District, students organized and taught a Saturday workshop on reciprocal teaching to faculty. They demonstrated the approach and talked about how it assisted them in their learning, pointing out how they learned from both teachers and each other. The teachers confirmed that learning and teaching are both reciprocal.

My 10-year-old granddaughter, Shannon, serves as a mediator at Longfellow School in Salida, Colorado. If she notices two 1st graders fighting over something, she and another mediator go over to the children, introduce themselves, and ask if they have a problem. If they say yes, the children are asked to describe the problem, their feelings and needs, and whether they can think of a solution. When the children arrive at their own solution, they shake hands and write down their names to give to the counselor as a record of success.

When Rosalinda Canlas served as an assistant principal in Newark, California, she and her colleagues implemented a conflict management program for 4th, 5th, and 6th graders in which students served as conflict managers (though teachers and parents were trained as well). The program resulted in reduced behavioral referrals and suspension—a 43 percent reduction in referrals the first year alone—increased effectiveness among students in solving problems, and parent interest in using conflict resolution strategies at home (Canlas, 1996).

A public commitment to student leadership has often been expressed through the establishment of governance opportunities. However, representation on boards and committees can be of a token nature (e.g., one or two students on a team or council), and student voices have not traditionally been a strong presence. In order for governance to be genuine, the following guidelines can be helpful:

- Select students for teams, councils, groups, and boards in much the same way as teacher representatives are selected (see Chapter 2). Ask students to identify criteria for participation, and invite nominations from them and

their peers. Select enough student representatives to have an authentic voice.
- Because student participation in decision making is developmental (see Figure 6.1), provide student mentoring through the decision-making process. It is important to meet with students before and after meetings to talk through the agenda and debrief roles and actions in the meeting.
- Connect student participation in governance with congruent school and classroom practices. If students are involved in democratic practices in a governance group but fail to have those same opportunities in other settings, all experiences may become inauthentic.

Student voice expressed through democratic experiences helps develop student learning and leadership. I would argue, in fact, that student voice is the most fundamental issue in student development.

Instructional Practices That Generate Student Leadership

Effective student learning is based upon the principles of constructivism that underlie human learning (see Figure 6.2). Constructivism, in turn, is based on an understanding of student voice and the need to ignite the brain and focus learning. Pondering ideas and interacting with others enables learners to construct their own meaning and shared knowledge. Meaning becomes most apparent to students when they learn from the literature and history of their own cultures, and is constructed as students make sense of the discrepancies between what they used to know and believe and what they are now experiencing. As with adults, inquiry and discovery are the primary means by which students find and create new knowledge. Self-assessment spurs reflection and the

FIGURE 6.1

The Role of Adolescents in the Decision-Making Process

Adolescents have no say in decisions that affect them.	Select group of adolescents has a voice in *student affairs.*	Adolescents have token *membership in adult groups.*	Adolescents *and adults* take a major-ity vote on decisions.	Adolescents and adults reach *consensus* on decisions.

Environment that inhibits adolescent leaders ⟶ Environment that encourages adolescent leaders

Source: Van Linden and Fertman (1998).

metacognition that translates and combines learning experiences into true learning. Programs that emphasize the design and development of thought from a constructivist perspective include *Habits of Mind* (Costa & Kallick, 2000), *Understanding by Design* (Wiggins & McTighe, 1998), and *Mosaic of Thought* (Keene & Zimmerman, 1997) among others.

Intrinsic motivation is another essential ele-ment of learning and development. While extrinsic motivation (like praise) can be an important part of a student's world, a predomi-nance of such motivation can make students overly dependent on the outside world and inhibit their development. Whether in a child or an adult, intrinsic motivation is deeply linked to maturing capabilities, identity, and cognitive complexity.

One of the central premises of the Child Development Project in Oakland, California, is an emphasis on intrinsic motivation as integral to healthy student development. The Project seeks to establish whole-school renewal and caring learning communities by integrating social and ethical principles into the curricu-lum and supporting collaborative classroom

learning, a classroom focus on problem-solving and responsibility, parent and family involve-ment, and a schoolwide culture of helpfulness. I have personally found that schools involved with the Child Development Project tend to accelerate and magnify the effects of leadership capacity. I suspect that this may be true because the principles apply just as well to students, teachers, and parents.

Student Resiliency

Schools that pursue student learning and lead-ing understand that resiliency is central to both. Students who are resilient are able to bounce back from adversity and resist being pulled into hopelessness by difficult environments. These students display self-direction, problem-solving capabilities, social competence, and participa-tion in the world around them; they also con-tribute to others and possess a sense of purpose and future.

Fortunately, resiliency is not a matter of birth or chance. Schools can provide their stu-dents with "protective factors" such as caring, high expectations, purposeful support, and

FIGURE 6.2
Principles of Constructivism

Constructivist learning can be distinguished from other learning theories by the following principles.

Knowledge and beliefs are formed within the learner. Rather than considering learners as "empty vessels," constructivist-learning theory assumes that learners bring experience and understandings to the classroom. Consequently they do not encounter new information out of context, but rather apply what they know to *assimilating* this information, or else accommodate what they know to match new insights. Either way, the process of knowledge acquisition is interactive.

Learners personally imbue experiences with meaning. The values and beliefs they have already formed help learners to interpret and assign meaning, as do their interactions with other students. Meaning is constructed and shaded by students' previous experiences. Thus two students reading the same poem will interpret the meaning of the poem's images first according to their individual schemas, and second by their interactions with the perspectives of other students.

Learning activities should cause learners to gain access to their experiences, knowledge, and beliefs. Constructivist approaches to learning include those that allow learners to use what they know to interpret new information and construct new knowledge. Questions posed to students should prompt their writing to connect with what they know and believe. When these connections are made, learners draw on what they know and reshape it in new and newly meaningful ways.

Culture, race, and economic status affect student learning individually and collectively. Student identities and origins affect their experiences both in and out of school. While it is important to incorporate these experiences into the learning, it is even more important to help students understand how their ethnicity and economic status affect them in school and beyond. Poor and minority students often get the message that they have not contributed to the history, literature, arts, or economics of their society because their experiences and accomplishments are not reflected in the formal curriculum.

Learning is a social activity that is enhanced by shared inquiry. Students learn with greater depth and understanding when they share ideas with others, engage in the dynamic and synergistic process of thinking together, consider other points of view, and broaden their own perspectives. Constructivism advances the idea that learning is a social endeavor requiring engagement with others in order to gain a growing understanding of the world and one's relationship to it.

Reflection and metacognition are essential to the construction of knowledge and meaning. Learners clarify their understandings when they are able to reflect on their learning and to analyze the ways they construct knowledge and meaning. Students develop as learners when they are aware of the processes they engage in as they "come to know." This awareness enhances their ability to learn and make sense of new information.

Learners play a critical role in assessing their own learning. Teachers traditionally establish learning goals and criteria for success and evaluate student progress. Student self-assessment makes the processes for learning explicit to students, shaping their personal schemas and enabling them to actively engage with new learning in the future.

The outcomes of the learning process are varied and often unpredictable. Since students help direct their own learning and generate both understanding and meaning, the teacher gives up a degree of control over both the process and outcomes. Student interpretations and perspectives may be richer than the teacher imagined and may take a different path than anticipated.

Note: Adapted from Walker (2002).

opportunities for meaningful participation and contribution (Krovetz, 1999). These factors can be expressed through looping in vertical communities (see the Kansas City example in Chapter 2), guidance programs, classrooms as bonded communities, high standards for all students, service learning, and student leadership. In Figure 6.3, John Kretzmann suggests "Ten Commandments" for involving young people in community building.

Smallness, Intimacy, and Community

My Kansas high school was attended by 90 students in four grades. We knew each other well, and more than 40 years later many of us still do. When there was a musical, everyone was in it; when there was a journalism project, everyone did it; when there was a reunion, everyone planned it. Opportunities for leadership abounded, and the close-knit community supported both our successes and our follies. I

FIGURE 6.3

"Ten Commandments" for Involving Young People in Community Building

By John P. Kretzmann

1. Always start with the gifts, talents, knowledge, and skill of young people—never with their needs and problems.
2. Always lift up the unique individual, never the category to which the young person belongs. It is "Frank, who sings so well" or "Maria, the great soccer player." Never the "at-risk youth" or the "pregnant teen."
3. Share the conviction that (a) every community is filled with useful opportunities for young people to contribute to the community, and (b) there is no community institution or association that can't find a useful role for young people.
4. Try to distinguish between real community building work, and games or fakes—because young people know the difference.
5. Fight—in every way you can—age segregation. Work to overcome the isolation of young people.
6. Start to get away from the principle of aggregation of people by their emptiness. Don't put everyone who can't read together in the same room. It makes no sense.
7. Move as quickly as possible beyond youth "advisory boards" or councils, especially those boards with only one young person on them.
8. Cultivate many opportunities for young people to teach and to lead.
9. Reward and celebrate every creative effort, every contribution made by young people. Young people can help take the lead here.
10. In every way possible, amplify this message to young people: *We need you!* Our community cannot be strong and complete without you.

Reprinted by permission.

wasn't much of a singer, but the audience applauded appreciatively. Our plays, chorus recitals, writing projects, and sports teams basked in the warmth of community support. We were coaxed into our better selves, and in return we gave back to the community.

My experience doesn't stand alone. Small schools (i.e., 400 students or less) and classes are places where teachers and students get to know one another, feel less anonymous, trust each other, and learn and work together (Meek, 2002; Wasley, 2002). Studies reveal that, as compared to large schools, small schools foster

- Up to 100 percent fewer dropouts;
- Higher grade point averages;
- Greater student and parent satisfaction;
- One-tenth of the correlation between poverty and low achievement;
- Fewer instances of violence; and
- Greater participation on the part of students and teachers (Wasley, 2002).

Meek (2002) reminds us that we must "organize our schools for *largeness of thought* while also promoting the *benefits of smallness:* familiarity in relationships, a sense of belonging, and a sense of community." Smallness doesn't create community in and of itself, but it can create the conditions in which personal and learning relationships can flourish. To care about others, we have to know them. If I know the name of your dog and your brother and what you like to do, I am less afraid of you, and I am less likely to bully you. Familiarity enables us to care about each other and to come to know ourselves in the process.

Reflection as Assessment of Learning and Leading

Reflection develops the inner voice into the public voice. It is a higher form of learning and an essential dimension of constructivist learning, for it is how we integrate what we are coming to know. As a form of assessment, reflection applies equally to learning and leading.

The experiential learning process of reflection—looking back at what you've learned, gaining useful insight from the analysis, and applying this new knowledge to daily work—helps students to understand the meaning and effect of their contributions (van Linden & Fertman, 1998). By including reflection time on meeting agendas, for instance, students learn that reflecting on their own actions is a way to regularly think about leading and learning.

Schools are increasingly using reflection tools for learning and to assess learning, whether in the form of portfolios, journals, dialogue, or products and performances resulting from problem-based learning. Rather than discussing only data relating to test scores, as is the norm these days, we need also to discuss data that emerges from reflection as legitimate measures of success and to include students in any dialogue.

So far, I have identified certain approaches to teaching and learning that engender both the capacity to learn and the capacity to lead. This list is not definitive, but it is a sampling of approaches that share the same essential assumptions: *student voice, constructivism, intrinsic motivation, resiliency, smallness,* and *reflection.* When put into practice, these assumptions work to promote higher levels of student leadership and, therefore, enhanced achievement.

Student Leadership Programs with Promise

Students who lead participate in and contribute to school. In January 2002, I visited some 2nd graders in Cupertino, California, who had designed and written beautiful placards proclaiming their own dreams. Each of the placards wished for the world to become a better place—

for peace, nonviolence, health, and love. The students' concerns for the world were remarkably uniform and compassionate. Yet I am often disappointed to see high school students who, driven by test performance, competition, and consumerism, lose sight of their 2nd grade dreams. As adults, we need to keep the spirit of compassion and contribution alive by attending to the skillful participation of students in the world around them.

I have noted above the important role of students in classroom communities, peer mediation, reciprocal learning with both students and adults, governance, and action research. New and equally compelling opportunities are arising

in school governance; wilderness experiences; antibias and ethical relationships, which are essential for mutual respect and understanding; and technology, which enhances our capacities for effective communication. Figure 6.4 summarizes some of the ways in which students demonstrate leadership.

Carlisle High School, in Carlisle, Pennsylvania, has a K–12 Leadership Academy built upon the assumption that all students have leadership skills and potential. The district coordinators, Debra Ferguson and Debra Hines, conducted focus groups with students in 2002 about their opportunities for leadership. The students opined that leadership opportunities were

FIGURE 6.4
Some Student Acts of Leadership

- Participating in community-building activities at the classroom and the school levels
- Service in peer assistance roles, including tutoring and teaching, mentoring, mediation, and facilitation
- Participating in conversations about student development and performance, contributing data of their own; self-assessment and reflection; individual goal-setting and planning
- Participating in decision-making and governance groups
- Advocating for schoolwide improvements
- Joining school research teams, which might include conducting focus groups with other students, parents, and community members
- Participating in curriculum and instructional practices such as library development, securing apprenticeships, and developing project-based learning activities
- Organizing and influencing other students to participate in the school community: for instance, improving curricular relevancy and designing processes for environmental improvement, mutual student support, peer counseling, and conflict management
- Participating in policymaking arenas and board meetings, speaking to issues of interest
- Resource development (e.g., advocating with businesses, assisting with grants, and influencing district budget decisions)
- Organizing and participating in parent/student/teacher conferences
- Setting program evaluation criteria and providing evaluative feedback

reserved for students engaged in activities—clubs, sports, and student council—available to only a few. Carlisle High now uses technology and an integrated leadership curriculum to make leadership available to all students by

- Allowing all students the opportunity to identify the characteristics of leadership and to serve in leadership capacities;
- Promoting ethics in relation to citizenship, leadership, and technology;
- Encouraging community and service learning; and
- Integrating the existing character education and antibias curriculum with Web activities. (For instance, studies of the Japanese Internment during World War II, the Civil Rights movement, and the Great Depression have led to community projects related to civil liberties and poverty.)

By their junior year, most students who intend to drop out actually do so. According to the staff at the Contra Costa (California) County Jail, incarcerated young adults report that the lure of available transportation, the press of peers to join gangs, irresistible sexual opportunities, and increasing demands to meet graduation requirements turned junior year into the time their lives fell apart.

Yet junior year can also be a time of transformation, when students are provided with challenging and life-affirming opportunities. At the Athenian School in Danville, California, juniors participate in the Athenian Wilderness Experience (AWE), a 25- to 26-day journey into Death Valley or the High Sierras. The students confront challenging terrain, weather, and living conditions (including three days alone); learn survival skills; engage in community living and ecological practices; and study natural history. Deep reflection is expected using group dialogue, journals, and readings. This carefully planned

and thoughtfully executed program is led by Arlene Ustin, who along with her colleagues believes that the junior year is a time of great passion for young people—perhaps the greatest they will ever encounter. If this passion is not tapped into, the school will fall short of its goals of promoting intellectual pursuit and a responsible citizenry.

According to Ustin, 23 years of observation and evaluation have established the transformational patterns inherent to AWE. She says the program allows students to develop

- A deep and active compassion,
- Maturation and self-confidence,
- A moral compass that guides decisions and behaviors,
- Skills for taking care of each other in a multicultural context,
- A perspective that helps them to understand the difference between necessity and privilege,
- Unique and emerging leadership qualities,
- Deepened reflective practices, and
- Clarity regarding their next steps in life.

Students of all ages can learn active compassion when their schools focus on student development and responsibility. In Chapter 2, we met the Dreamkeepers, an equity advocacy team at Garfield School in San Leandro, California. Each year, 40 out of the school's 150 4th and 5th grade students form the Garfield Gator Guardians (GGG). The GGG serve as trained conflict mediators and classroom leaders, lend their voices to action research, and host visitors to the school. The team members know the school well and interpret their knowledge for other students and adults. In 2002, the GGG's influence on the school has been remarkable: discipline referrals have been cut by a third (and suspensions by half), and GGG members who were having difficulty themselves learn to behave as role models for others.

Springvale South Primary School in Melbourne, Australia, focuses on "Engagement and Connectedness" as a framework for involving students in all forms of community life. The school is highly diverse, with many languages spoken among students. Principal Lyn Watts ascribes her student's high achievement to the expression of student voice and leadership, setting goals with students, and including students' interests in the curriculum. In addition, students evaluate their own performance and engage in action research, which has also resulted in improved achievement. During the past year, staff members focused on the reading achievement of boys and ESL students. They studied the effects of their new approaches, and discovered that reading comprehension rose by more than 100 percent for boys and 300 percent for students with non–English speaking backgrounds, as measured on the Torch test.

Conclusion

Learning and leading cannot be separated: leading is a form of learning together. Instructional programs that evoke student voice, apply the principles of constructivism, attend to intrinsic motivation, build resiliency, and engage students in democratic governance—all within a small context, whether natural or contrived—develop the leadership capacity of students.

So far in this book, we have seen that teachers, administrators, and students develop in similar ways. In Chapter 7, I will discuss how similar developmental principles can be applied to parents transitioning from simple involvement to participation and finally to leadership.

Questions and Activities

1. Discuss the following questions in small groups in a team or faculty meeting: How has this chapter informed you about the focus of your own work? How has it helped you better understand your school's gaps in student achievement, instruction, and school practices?

2. Form a question rooted in this chapter's key concepts, such as:

- How is your behavior aligned with the key ideas in this chapter?
- Where can alignment be strengthened?
- What does good teaching and learning look like in our classes?
- How resilient are our students? How do we know that?
- Is our school too big and impersonal? What might we do to create "smallness"?
- Are our students working as leaders in our school community? What evidence do we have?

Conduct small group dialogues (see Chapter 3 for guidelines) on these questions.

3. Have teams of teachers, students, and parents design a focus group study of randomly selected students from across grade levels. Focus group questions could include the following:

- What does it mean to be a leader at school?
- Would you describe yourself as a leader? Why or why not?
- Has there been a time when you performed as a leader? Give us an example.
- What might we do to increase or improve student leadership in our school community?

4. Review Figure 6.4 in small groups or teams. Place a plus sign (+) beside the acts of student leadership that take place in your school. Compare your findings with those of the other teams, and discuss additional steps that your school might take to expand student leadership.

5. If resiliency is not a familiar concept in your school, secure an article or book on the

topic (see References) and read it. Form a study group around the concept.

6. In a faculty or team meeting, brainstorm on chart paper your most prevalent approaches to classroom management and school discipline. List practices that rely on intrinsic motivation on one side of the paper and those that rely on extrinsic motivation on the other side. Discuss. Place an action item on the next agenda to consider actions that will move your school toward more frequent use of intrinsic motivation.

7. In the classroom, ask students to reflect upon the contributions they make toward others. Ask them to write their responses as a journal entry that you may share with other teachers. Select a range of responses: at least one entry that shows considerable reflection and understanding, one that shows moderate reflection and understanding, and one that shows little reflection. Take these entries to a team or faculty meeting and share as student work. Ask yourselves how you might improve student reflection.

CHAPTER 7
Parents as Leaders

Talking about parents as leaders is different from discussing parent *involvement.* The latter term conjures up images of parents volunteering at school, showing interest in their own children, fund raising, and reading the latest newsletter. These are all important activities, but they fall short of true parent leadership, in which parents

- **Colead** with children, teachers, administrators, and other parents with respect to all the students at the school;
- **Participate** in education practices with others in the school community;
- **Advocate** education to other parents, community, and policymakers; and
- **Assume** collective responsibility for the learning of all children.

The educators at Belvedere School surprised even themselves when they observed a shift in their perspectives about parents. Determined to extend to parents the same regard and opportunities for reciprocity that they extend to students and each other, Jennifer and her colleagues sought to reexamine traditional parent roles in their school. During one intense dialogue session, they discussed their current and potential views of parents (see Figure 7.1).

The staff members were keen to revise their approach to parental involvement in part because they were determined to eliminate tracking and remedial programs at Belvedere in favor of integrated, differentiated instruction: they were certain that they would need parent support for such a change, and were startled at the conflicting agendas and strong opinions among parents. The staff members confronted some tough realities. By viewing parents as customers, they had sought to provide them only

Figure 7.1
Parents as Partners

Traditional Roles	Reciprocal Roles
Customers to be satisfied	Partners to be engaged
Servants to the school	Collaborators with faculty and staff
Obstacles to change	Facilitators of change
Critics to be persuaded	Colearners
Students of parenting	Coteachers
Audience for staff decisions and actions	Decision makers with staff
Fund raisers	Resource developers
Clerks and carpenters	Team members

with good information about the school and "protected" them from struggling with tough problems, which were sometimes characterized by unsatisfactory student achievement. Information had flown in a single direction, verbally as well as in writing. In turn, the school expected unquestioned loyalty and service, and was often disappointed by a lack of parent enthusiasm.

To fully ensure a reciprocal role for parents necessitated some important shifts in thinking. Parents could be expected to join the Belvedere team as *partners,* with all the concomitant responsibilities and privileges. Viewing them as coleaders and colearners meant that everyone had much to learn from everyone else and that educators need not hide information from them that was not yet fully developed or might not be wholly positive. Such transparency enabled staff to relax and ask genuine questions in the presence of parents. By the time Jennifer became principal she could look to parents as well as

staff to hold a broad view of Belvedere's commitment to and responsibility for the learning of all children.

The Role of Parents in Schools at Different Stages of Leadership Capacity

In a Quadrant 1 school, the few parents who are involved with the school may have one primary agenda: to attain the most suitable placement and experience for their own children, often by demanding placement in a specific teacher's classroom. Most parent voices are either silent or heard only when the parent is called to school because of a discipline problem or special-education placement.

In a Quadrant 2 school, more parents are involved in some aspects of school life, often attached to a specific program—sports, for instance, or the performing arts. There is little overall involvement or clarity about participation options in the school as a whole.

In a Quadrant 3 school, involved parents are more skillful and focused in their participation and have begun to exhibit shared responsibility for the school's improvement. Though most parents may remain on the outside or be more superficially involved, the school recognizes improved parent participation as an important goal.

In a Quadrant 4 school, we see the emergence of true parent leadership as discussed in this chapter. It should be noted that even in a school that is improving rapidly, parent leadership may be the last arena to be addressed.

The Struggle for Collective Responsibility

One of the most challenging aspects of schooling is the struggle to develop collective responsibility among parents. Parents—particularly affluent ones, who often have inordinate influence in the school community—are notorious for supporting program approaches that

- Separate and label children so that students are in classes with others like themselves (or like the parents' image of them),
- Erect competitive structures so that some students win and many others lose, and
- Use more traditional instructional and assessment practices that confuse information with knowledge and test results for the presence of knowledge (Kohn, 1998). (Most standardized tests measure the accumulation of information rather than knowledge; in order for information to become knowledge, it must be imbued with meaning and be available for application.)

In a highly competitive society, it is understandable that parents want their own children to get the best scores so that they can attend the best colleges and acquire the best jobs. In the few years since Kohn (1998) wrote his exposé of parents as obstructionists to school improvement, the national press for individual achievement has if anything worsened, and the breadth of curriculum and assessment approaches has narrowed.

Our task as courageous leaders is to help parents understand that a handful of individuals armed with high test scores does not constitute a democratic society. At the same time, parents must feel confident that their own children are not sacrificed for the good of the rest; schools must improve for the benefit of all their students.

We begin to negotiate this challenge with the development of reciprocity, which requires a maturity of perspective that usually emerges from opportunities to participate in communities over time. We must enlarge the circle of community to be more inclusive than in the past if we are to develop reciprocal partnerships with parents and members of the broader community. Together we can improve learning for children and adults, but it requires from educators the confidence that emerges from broad-based, skillful participation. Lack of such confidence can lead to holding parents at arm's length or mechanized interactions with those outside the school.

As Belvedere School discovered, school relationships with parents and the community are notoriously nonreciprocal: typically, neither group expresses full regard for the other. A few examples:

- Parents are recruited to *serve the school* (sponsor fund raisers, work in classrooms, donate time to school beautification, and set up for the science fair)
- Social agencies are called on in emergencies to handle problems that the school is unequipped to deal with

- Student outcomes may include community-related goals, but usually as a means for students to meet their own goals only
- Businesses contribute to the school only as a function of their charitable work
- Other schools, regional education agencies, and professional networks approach the school only when it hosts particular programs or can provide training on certain subjects
- Universities seek out the school to conduct research on human subjects

In the first three examples, the school seeks to "use" parents, agencies, and communities to strengthen the perceived welfare of the school; in the other three, the school itself is used as an object of charity, expertise, and research. These are not necessarily negative practices to be avoided, but they lack the learning power of more reciprocal relationships.

The pursuit of reciprocity presents us with some key questions:

- What does each entity have to give and to receive?
- What do they each have to learn from each other?
- What knowledge can these partners construct together, thereby creating something that did not exist before and that each had to learn?

These questions suggest that we have as much to learn from parents as they have to learn from us, and that together we can figure things out more effectively than we could separately. I personally am of the belief, derived from experience, that parents who participate in conversations about schooling develop a broad perspective that enables them to honor their own values, remain vigilant regarding their own children, and advocate for and help create successful schools for all.

In order to develop a parent community that leads, participates, advocates, and assumes collective responsibility, we can consider the following guidelines:

- **State explicitly your school's high expectations of parent participation.** Why not describe parent leadership in public forums and written communications?
- **Engage parents in developing a shared vision.** Provide forums in which parents are asked to discuss their deepest hopes for all students.
- **Make learning transparent.** Keep classrooms open for visitations, hold "walk throughs" with parents, discuss how learning occurs and how it can be recognized, and conduct public exhibitions of student work.
- **Establish relationships that are reciprocal in purpose and behavior.** For instance, hold conferences that explore how children learn at home and what this means for learning in the classroom. Each encounter should enable both the parents to be better at parenting and the school to be better at teaching.
- **Develop structures and processes for parent-to-parent leadership and advocacy.** For example, design phone trees for opinion polling, conduct focus group studies, and inform parents about new learning practices. Ask parents to exchange services.
- **Assume that parents have the right, responsibility, and ability to struggle with tough issues.** (See Chapter 8 for the policy on problem solving.)
- **Keep parent participation broad-based.** Do whatever it takes to involve parents widely (e.g., language translation, evening/weekend gatherings, baby-sitting, providing food). Otherwise, affluent and single-agenda parents may dominate the conversation.
- **Ask parents to assess their own leadership skills.** Hold conversations about parent

leadership, ask parents to write reflective statements about their own leadership, and survey parents about leadership behaviors.

These guidelines are designed to establish parent leadership in the school. The examples below are drawn from schools and districts that have altered their relationships with parents and therefore their capacity to lead and sustain school improvement.

Programs That Promote Parent Leadership

My own experiences with parent groups and councils over the years have led me to believe that when parents are fully engaged in the substantive conversations of schooling, they, like teachers, become more fully who they are. I have often worked with parents in retreats to develop visions and goals and train them in leadership skills. These experiences afforded educators and parents the opportunities to get to know each other, share our aspirations for students, and help construct new ways of thinking about student learning. The following examples are drawn from schools, districts, and regions that seek and value parent leadership.

Chapelfield Elementary School in Gahanna, Ohio, has created a remarkable program in which parents, along with other adult volunteers, learn to be constructivist teachers. Third grade teacher Mary Marquardt and Principal Barbara Murdock noticed that many 3rd graders were confused by the comprehension strategies needed for reading and writing, so they decided to launch a new kind of community of learners. Volunteers were trained to understand three things: the constructivist nature of learning, that the transfer of learning depends upon the scaffolding of learning by a more knowledgeable other, and that learning is recursive, occurring again and again. Working together each day

over a 10-day period, teams of three (two children and one adult) read a nonfiction book together, wrote about it, and discussed its structure and meaning over and over again. "Through conversation back and forth, students use their own language as the tool with which to craft new understandings together with old," said Marquardt. "The conversation with the adult volunteer is critical, because it is the vehicle through which children learn." These adults now better understand learning and how to care for other people's children as well as their own.

The mission of the Manitoba Association of Parent Councils (MAPC) is to "support, promote, and enhance meaningful parental involvement and participation in their advisory roles at the school, division, and provincial level." My observation is that MAPC members demonstrate parental leadership from the school to the provincial-policy level by discussing and advocating for such issues as equity, funding, discipline, special needs, standards, and parent involvement. The "Advocacy Project" enables parents and students to address tough issues and problems and advocate for solutions using processes available within the school system. In this specially designed parent education program, participants develop problem-resolution skills so that they may serve as effective advocates for children.

Public exhibitions offer outstanding examples of educators' work with parents. Parents and community members come to school events, usually in the spring, to witness student performances and products and to discuss the progress of performance improvement initiatives. Sherman Oaks Community Charter School in Campbell, California, holds events in which parents and students examine and discuss student work together: the students create passports for their parents, who attend public exhibitions of the students' study of countries. For this evening event, students are required to learn about their designated country, prepare products for the exhibition, and develop skills in communicating their learning to parents.

Mary Jo Pettigrew, principal of Indian Valley School, in Walnut Creek, California, organizes a major community event in the spring in which parents and community members participate in a protocol conversation around student work and other evidence of student achievement. For instance, in a protocol conversation regarding student performance on standardized tests, participants would display test results, discuss planned intervention and support strategies, and receive reflective feedback and questions.

Some of the most helpful conversations I have experienced have been in schools in which parent-teacher conferences were thoughtfully organized and planned through advisement programs. These types of conferences have become increasingly common over the past five years. Here is a small portion of one such conversation (Emil is the student):

> **Emil:** I want to thank you both for coming to this conference today. Let me show you some of my work and tell you how I think I'm doing.
>
> **Parent:** I'm very eager to see it. Do you have any examples of your writing?
>
> **Emil:** Yes, here are two samples that I think are a "4" on the rubric.
>
> **Parent:** What is a rubric?
>
> **Emil:** A rubric tells me what good work looks like.
>
> **Teacher:** Our writing rubric has four columns for four levels of work. Here is an example. Emil, why don't you read your mother the fourth column on creativity?
>
> [*Emil reads.*]
>
> **Parent:** I like that! May I have a copy at home? I can see several ways that we might use it.
>
> **Teacher:** Certainly, this will be your copy.

Emil's mother felt increasingly competent in using multiple measures in understanding her son's work (Lambert et al., 2002).

At Douglas Harkness Community School in Calgary, Canada, parent conferences signal to parents that they are respected partners in the learning process. According to principal Annie Davies, a study of parent attitudes about conferencing revealed that they would like to be presented with a choice of conferencing formats. On the first day of conferencing, student-led conferences allow students to share their work with parents; on the second day, parents may schedule one-on-one conferences with their students' teachers.

The Lagunitas Elementary School District in Marin County, California, has a successful 30-year history of offering parents a wide array of alternative programs, all of which are led by a council of parents and teachers. School staff members help families choose wisely among an "Open Program," a "Public Montessori Program," and a more traditional "Academics and Enrichment" alternative. Members of the program council, which is based upon mutual respect and equality between teachers and parents, have authority over governance and instructional decision making. Each program typically has at least one unofficial advocate on the local school board. The former superintendent of Lagunitas, Morgan Dale Lambert, reports that his major challenges—from which he derived great professional satisfaction—were mediating among empowered advocates, ensuring equity and coherence, and interpreting the complex and creative enterprise of school choice to other educators at local, county, and state levels.

Teachers at Glassbrook Elementary School were not persuaded that parents held high expectations for their children. In the highly mobile and diverse community of Hayward, California, parents seemed to leave their children at the school door without contributing much to their education and care. So the staff at Glassbrook, no longer satisfied with assumptions, developed an inquiring stance. At one faculty meeting, a teacher asked: "What do we really know to be true about parent expectations for their children?" This question stimulated the faculty to conduct surveys and conversations with parents, which produced surprising results: for example, 90 percent of the parents expected their children to go to college. This finding led to the creation of Parent University, in which parents and faculty could learn about topics important to both (e.g., new research in child development or technology).

At the New Century Learning Center in the Los Angeles Unified School District, parents don't need to be able to understand English in order to fully participate. Principal Yvonne Chan and her colleagues expect all parents to be involved. The district's Parent Exchange Service Bank is a unique, reciprocal means for parents to provide service to each other. "One person does child care so someone else can come to school," says Chan. "If you are sick, someone can walk your kindergartner to school. Everyone has to give" (Chan, 1999).

The site council in the Hickman Community Charter District, a small rural district in California, established the Family Resource Center in 1994 as a place where parents and volunteers could help students, teachers, and other parents. Jeanette Orth, the Center's parent involvement coordinator since its founding, reports that the center allows parents to learn new skills together and build confidence and self-direction in a learning environment that encourages them to experiment. Such confidence has led parents to exhibit both advocacy and leadership for all children in the district: parents have launched the district's Governor's Reading Program, for instance, which significantly increased the amount of monthly reading among students, and have

also tutored students, taught teachers artistic skills, and networked with other parents. According to Orth, "There seems to be a silent message of importance when a person spends time doing something to help someone else with no compensation" (personal communication, 2002).

The Commonwealth Institute for Parent Leadership in Kentucky is a pioneering effort designed to help parents become activists for student achievement. Parent participants are recruited from all over the state to attend seminars about standards-based systems for children and design projects aimed at improving student achievement. The projects must focus on improving student achievement, increasing parent involvement, and having a lasting effect. For instance, at Noe Middle School in Louisville, parents organized a program to help incoming 6th graders and their parents adjust to the school. The program has since grown to include all grade levels, expanded parent involvement, and improved student behavior and sense of community (Henderson & Raimondo, 2001).

The Saratoga School District, a highly affluent community near San Francisco, is made up largely of upper-middle-class parents, many of whom display the attitudes that Alfie Kohn warned us about. Superintendent Mary Gardner (personal communication, 2002) tells a story that shows how collective responsibility can be unearthed when parents are fully involved in the study and development of educational improvements. According to Gardner, the district's gifted and talented program had been subject to much parent criticism. In response the district formed a task force composed of students who were in the program and parents whose children were not. The parents spent a year examining new research about gifted instruction and inclusion and equity issues, collecting anecdotes about their experiences from parents, and visiting classrooms and exemplary programs. At the end of the year, the task force recommended to the school board that

- All students be identified as gifted and talented;
- The "pullout" program, which was based on an IQ measure of academic ability, be eliminated;
- Identification and instruction for all students be based on Howard Gardner's theory of multiple intelligences; and
- Waivers be secured from the state department of education in order for the program to move forward.

Today, *every* student in Saratoga is gifted.

Conclusion

The schools, districts, and organizations described in this chapter set about to develop parent leadership in the education of their own and other people's children, establish an advocacy/ activist stance toward education, and build collective responsibility. The remarkable promise of these initiatives is analogous to the success of the 90/90/90 schools (see Chapter 6): if it can be achieved in one school or community, it can be done in others as well.

Questions and Activities

1. Consider the idea of parent leadership as discussed in this chapter in a small-group teacher-parent dialogue.

2. Reread the conversation about parents at Belvedere School. In a faculty meeting, hold a similar conversation by considering how parent participation might be described if you shifted your perspective to a parents-as-partners stance. What, if any, new initiatives does this exercise suggest?

3. Ask parents to ask themselves the following questions at a meeting, through a survey, or in a focus group:

- How do I participate in my child's school community?
- In what ways do I engage other parents in the school community?
- Do I help our school be successful with all children, especially those who are most vulnerable? If so, how?
- Do I advocate for education with local, regional, and state policy makers? What approaches might help me to do so more effectively?
- What additional knowledge and skills would help me to be an even better parent leader?

4. In small dialogue groups, consider the concept of collective parental responsibility. Consider whether or not there is evidence that parents feel collective responsibility for the learning of all children.

5. Read and discuss Figure 7.2. What would you add to this list? What would you like to try?

6. Design the agenda for your next parent council meeting. Send a copy of this chapter out with the agenda. Include a time to discuss how the guidelines in item three above might affect the council's work.

FIGURE 7.2
Acts of Parent Leadership

- Contributing data of their own to conversations about student development and performance
- Participating in decision making, planning, and development
- Joining school research teams, which might include conducting focus groups with other parents and community members
- Participating in curriculum and instructional practices such as securing apprenticeships and developing project-based learning
- Organizing and influencing other parents to participate
- Advocating for school programs
- Influencing policymakers on behalf of students and schools
- Developing resources (e.g., advocating with businesses, assisting with grants, and influencing district budget decisions)
- Organizing and participating in parent/student/teacher conferences
- Helping to set program evaluation criteria and providing evaluative feedback

CHAPTER 8
Time for Leadership

Unyielding and relentless, the time available in a uniform six-hour day and a 180-day year is the unacknowledged design flaw in American education. By relying on time as the metric for school organization and curriculum, we have built a learning enterprise on a foundation of sand. . . .

—National Education Commission on Time and Learning (1994, p. 8)

Time is understandably a problem in our profession. Our society has unwisely scrunched a full year's job into eight months, and filled a professional day with too many students, disciplines, classes, and duties. What is an educator to do? How do we find the time to build leadership capacity in our schools and districts?

In the grand scheme of things, we need a longer school year, fewer students and disciplines each day, and more time for collegial work. While advocating for these policies, however, we must deal with the here and now. In this chapter I will ask you to think somewhat differently about time—to find it, create it, and come to terms with what we can do while still maintaining healthy sensibilities and relationships.

Imprisoned by Time

Time is a tyrant that controls our lives: It hides from us, steals from us, and eats up the space that surrounds us. We feel most victimized by time when

- There are so many tasks and agendas that we feel pulled in many directions and helpless to change our conditions;
- Our meetings are ineffective and we leave feeling more tired than when we began;
- There are no decision-making processes, leading to inertia;
- Mandates disrupt our work and cause us to change direction; and
- We work hard but do not feel successful.

These are the feelings that we experience in a school with low leadership capacity. Genuine and skillful participation is lacking, there is little shared sense of purpose or focus, we cannot find a rationale for our actions, and we do not avail ourselves of opportunities to reflect. Most of all, we feel increasingly unsuccessful at the one thing we are here to do: teach students well.

Quadrant 4 Time

The teachers in Jennifer's school don't talk about time much anymore. I find that educators in Quadrant 4 schools talk less about time because they talk less about barriers in general. Sometimes they have more time allotted for collegial purposes than do Quadrant 1, 2, or 3 schools, but usually they have come to think of and experience time differently than in schools with lower leadership capacity.

When people have authentic relationships with each other, focus on a shared purpose, and work effectively and efficiently, they create a new form of energy. We sometimes call it *synergy:* a form of fellowship that regenerates energy rather than draining it. We feel calmer, clearer, and less harried by internal conflict about the choices that we make. Synergy in schools arises from conversations, collegial work, and action; it is the by-product of true collegiality.

Synergy is heightened during extended periods of time, such as daylong sessions and multiple-day retreats. In anthropology, the concept of "liminality" tells us that when we drop our assigned roles, usual dress, and expectations, as we do during retreats, we get to know ourselves and others in new ways. Things are never quite the same again after we've had such experiences: we relate to each other in deeper and more authentic ways, and listen to and appreciate others more. These encounters serve both as gifts to the community and to strengthen our *sense* of community.

When a certain level of synergy is reached in Quadrant 4 schools, individuals begin to cluster spontaneously into groups. They find time to be together, grouping and regrouping based on the work to be done, so that the principal doesn't have to convene all meetings. The following comments become commonplace: "Let's talk about this at lunch." "When can we meet?" "Let's gather in my room half an hour before school tomorrow." "How about Friday after school?"

The Clayton, Missouri, School District deliberately built on this concept of self-organization. Linda Henke, former assistant superintendent of the district, explains:

> We decided to push ourselves further and try an experiment in self-organizing. All district and school level staff members were put in charge of their own learning. . . . The staff was encouraged to form learning teams aligned with the district's goals (Panasonic Foundation, 1999, p. 9).

In Quadrant 4 schools, shared purpose, inquisitiveness, and reflection constitute the framework for synergy and self-organization, both of which help us think about and experience time in a different way. Before we can do this, however, we have to *find* time.

Finding Time

I could make the case that time isn't really the issue. After all, no matter what our occupation—be it president, pope, or prisoner—our day is composed of the same 24 hours. If we all had the same amount of money, money would be practically irrelevant. So the real issue is how we *decide to use* our time.

Most of us seem to find the time to do the things we think are important. Many schools and districts have been quite creative about finding more time when they realize it's necessary to achieve their student and adult learning goals.

The first place to look for time is in the areas that you share with your coworkers. The ZCI process described in Chapter 2, for instance, redistributes some of the tasks that gobble up time, thereby creating more time on the agenda for other, more important items. Similarly, the 30-minute meetings recommended by Conzemius and O'Neill impose both efficiency and quality to your work. (See Chapter 2 for a discussion of both of these approaches.)

Keeping essential questions about student learning in mind at all times allows us to focus our moment-to-moment interactions with each other. Staff members need to develop effective norms and guidelines for team meetings so that war stories and chitchat do not eat away at your precious time together. Do not use faculty meetings to disseminate information—use e-mail, personal contact, minutes, announcements, and policies instead. Removing items or tasks from your plate can make room for others. Though teachers are sometimes reluctant to let go of comfortable but time-consuming practices, these changes will be well worth the effort.

Imagine that you are a participant in the James Short Memorial School protocol on literacy described in Chapter 3. Think of the pleasure of exploring ideas and constructing knowledge together—all during work hours. When we allow time for reflective conversations, what is important becomes clearer to us. By choosing to integrate such conversations into our faculty or professional development meeting, we develop synergy and deepen our commitment to each other.

Finding new time during the day, though challenging, is necessary. When I was principal at San Jose Middle School in Novato, California, we created a "late start" day on Wednesday morning. We began by rotating responsibilities for preparing breakfast at around 7:30 and met until the buses arrived around 9:50 (yes, rescheduling the buses was difficult, but

solvable). During this time we held in-depth dialogues about teaching and learning, including discussion of strategies that we found successful as evidenced by student performance. Other schools use early dismissal one afternoon a week, professional time created by substitutes or specialists, and learning days—full days when students do not come to school—to hold dialogues.

The master schedule is a goldmine for finding new time. High schools with block schedules can find 90 minutes of collegial time on alternate days, during which core teams can also meet. (Staff members who share the same preparation period might also form multidiscipline study teams.) Daily schedules can even be extended by 10 to 15 minutes to accommodate a longer collegial period once a week. Barkley (1999) proposes the creation of 15-hour blocks of planning time during a given week, for which purpose faculty members are divided into two groups. In the morning, half the teachers teach a quality-learning seminar to all of the students; in the afternoon, the other half teaches them. This type of quarterly commitment to making time can add depth to any school's professional development program.

At Creekside School in the Black Mine School District, California, teams of substitutes—many of them parent volunteers—prepare and teach a particular curriculum focus while teachers have a full day to examine student work. The staff members at Creekside, which is a self-governing school, refer to these sessions as Directed Academic Study (DAS) days. Many schools use special funding to buy teacher time in the summer for in-depth work such as the development of standards-based language arts units. Many highly successful networks, such as the National Writing Project and many graduate programs, are held during the summer.

At Englehard School in Louisville, Kentucky, students do not attend school on Fridays. Staff members decided to lengthen the school year in order to reserve 20 percent of their week for professional time. This decision, along with the many others that resulted in a professional culture and shared leadership, led to outstanding student achievement (Lambert et al., 2002).

Sherman Oaks Community Charter School in Campbell, California, provides 90 minutes of professional time per day. The time is composed of lunch, an activity, and a reading period, all supervised by both instructional aides and parents. Staff members have resisted the temptation to use some of this time for business, which is handled either personally or by e-mail; instead, the time is used to examine student work and other data, leading to improved teaching practice.

Technology is particularly helpful when we're looking to find new time: online projects (which can be done at any time during the week), e-mail communication, and videotaped class presentations or coaching lessons allow our schedules greater flexibility. Once you start thinking more creatively about time, new arrangements will present themselves.

Lessons I've Learned About Time

In the many years I have spent as an educator and working with thousands of principals, teachers, students, and parents, I've learned the following lessons about time:

- **Time belongs to us.** It is a precious resource that we give as a gift to the endeavors and people we believe in.
- **Free time can be created from squandered time.** Since we all have the same *amount* of time, we must reexamine our assumptions about priorities in order to find time for important things. This process is a continuous archaeological dig.

- **When we spend time with others, we create synergy.** When we work well with others, time flies—and the flight is soothing.
- **It is essential to reserve time for ourselves.** Without personal time we lose focus and can overlook what's important in our rush to take care of what's "urgent."
- **Time is content-free.** The passage of time alone does not create change; what we *do with the time* does.
- **Time away from school results in a shift in perspective.** I often find that after the winter holidays—18 months into the process of building leadership capacity—responsibilities and relationships seem to realign themselves.
- **Time is essential to achieve anything of importance.**

Conclusion

The development of leadership capacity—or indeed any worthwhile endeavor—cannot be achieved without time. A few years ago I heard a wandering actor observe that in his experience, people consistently yearn for two things: to be in authentic relationships with others and to slow down. I've made the same observation, regardless of what line of work people are in. We must slow down in order to form relationships and achieve what matters most in the lives of children and adults.

Questions and Activities

1. Hold a dialogue (but not a discussion) about time at a staff meeting. Seek to understand how others feel about this issue and how they have come to terms with it in their lives. At the next meeting, list all the ways in which you can find time, and the items you can safely remove from your plate. Choose one new approach to finding time and implement it.

2. At a staff meeting, have everyone agree on the most important goal in the school according to the school's vision and plan. Consider whether the most important goal receives the most important time at the school. If not, explore ways to rectify the situation.

3. When planning for the next faculty meeting or for your leadership team's professional development day, pay particular attention to how time is used. Will the agenda go out ahead of *time?* Have you built in substantial *time* for the most important item? Have you taken the *time* to include a reflective conversation such as a dialogue or protocol? Have you allowed *time* for feedback from a process observer? Have you provided *time* for follow-up?

4. At a staff or team meeting, begin by asking everyone to write briefly on how best they used time that week. Discuss in pairs and share. What did you notice about the criteria individuals used for "the best use of time"? Discuss.

5. At a staff or team meeting, distribute three Post-It notes to each person, with each note representing one hour. On the wall, create headings such as "Team Meetings," "Individual Planning," "Sharing Instructional Ideas," "Collaborative Planning," "Tutoring Students," "Planning with Parents," "Meeting with Other Schools," "Collegial Dialogue," "Coaching," and so on. Ask individuals to stick their Post-It notes under the items to which they would most like to give their time. Observe the patterns and discuss in small groups, then in the larger group.

6. Have half the teachers at the school plan a three-hour learning workshop for students in an area of intense teacher interest and expertise. Each workshop should contain twice as many students as a regular classroom. The other group of teachers should reserve this time for collaborative planning and coaching. Reverse the process when the three hours are over, and evaluate its efficacy and quality at your next staff meeting.

CHAPTER 9
District Leadership

The most confounding question I've been asked might be the following: "Our school is moving toward Quadrant 4, but our district is still in Quadrant 1. What can we do?" I usually respond with a joke: "Build a moat around the school and fill it with bloodthirsty alligators."

I used to believe that the school was the primary unit of educational change, and the literature repeatedly insists that it is. However, I'm now persuaded that we can't save education one school at a time. Excellent schools in poor districts implode over time, whereas poor schools in excellent districts get better.

This chapter is designed to help achieve excellence in districts. The district Leadership Capacity Matrix (Figure 9.1), adapted from the school matrix (Figure 1.3), will frame the discussion.

The District Leadership Capacity Matrix

A district needs to develop not only its own leadership capacity, but that of its schools as well. This dual responsibility requires district administrators to model certain leadership behaviors; to abide by certain structures, processes, and policies; and to focus (and focus others) on student learning.

As you read the following district matrix scenarios, keep in mind that, as with schools, no one organization fits neatly into any box. Consider these scenarios representative of a tendency to act in a particular way depending on the district's breadth of participation and depth of skillfulness in the work of leadership. Most districts will actually display characteristics of all four quadrants.

FIGURE 9.1
District Leadership Capacity Matrix

	Low Degree of Participation	High Degree of Participation
Low Degree of Skill	• District managers are autocratic • Actions are derived from external directives rather than shared vision • Top-down accountability systems emphasize compliance and standardization (i.e., districts hand directives to schools, and schools report results to districts) • Direction is centralized in the form of mandates, resources, and rules and regulations, resulting in dependency relationships • Professional development is erratic and one-size-fits-all • Student achievement is low or directly correlated with ethnicity and socioeconomic status	• District managers take a laissez-faire approach • Because shared vision is lacking, there is fragmentation and poor program coherence within and among schools • Schools and individual teachers design assessment with minimal systemic use of information and evidence for accountability and improvement • Direction is decentralized and school-based, with little emphasis on coordination or coherence • Professional development is a potpourri of unrelated training choices • Student achievement varies widely among district schools—some are doing well while others show little or no improvement
High Degree of Skill	• District administrators delegate some authority and resources to schools with trained leadership teams • District and school visions are coordinated • District and school leadership teams develop lateral accountability systems, but without broad engagement • Coordination is generally close, with greater autonomy for schools with skillful leadership teams • Professional development is focused on district vision and goals • Student achievement and development are improving and gaps among groups are narrowing	• District administrators model, develop, and support broad-based, skillful participation in the work of leadership • Shared vision results in districtwide program coherence • An inquiry-based accountability system informs decision making and practice at classroom, school, and district levels • Organizational relationships involve high district engagement and low bureaucratization • During professional selection and development, administrators recruit and educate learners and leaders in partnership with schools • Student achievement and development are high or steadily improving in all schools, with equitable outcomes for all students

The Quadrant 1 District

In a Quadrant 1 district, administrators make and communicate decisions from the district office. These decisions are not derived from a vision of student learning, but rather in large part from state directives or political pressures. Schools are informed of performance expectations, which are usually linked to raising standardized test scores, and are expected to use whatever means possible to meet these targets. Mandates and rules bind, direct, and control most actions, including teacher hiring, textbook orders, and time and resource management. District professional development may be absent or erratic; when present, it usually emphasizes training without practice, observation, or coaching, and is often tied to a one-size-fits-all philosophy: for instance, the district may mandate a scripted reading program and deliver the same texts and training to all teachers regardless of competence or experience.

Relationships in Quadrant 1 districts are typically dependent or hostile. Directives and compliance expectations are met with silence or parking lot grousing. Conversations that describe negative conditions or complaints occur within small groups of principals. Problem solving rarely occurs at the district or school level. One of the saddest consequences of the Quadrant 1 district is that principals are expected to lead their schools the way the administrators lead the district; maverick schools seeking innovative approaches to improvement may be brought into line by being assigned a more controlling principal.

Student achievement is understandably low in this type of district; if there are improvements on test scores as a result of new initiatives, they are for the short term. Scores are predictably correlated with race, ethnicity, and socioeconomic status. Student development behaviors regarding attendance, retention, bullying, resiliency, and engagement remain problematic.

Superintendents in Quadrant 1 districts may not understand that their authoritarian approach will govern adult and student performance, and will tend to increase controls when targets are not met. The only hope is that the superintendents experience major epiphanies or leave their posts, or that the school board and community intervenes.

The Quadrant 2 District

The Quadrant 2 district is characterized by a somewhat laissez-faire approach to management. District support for schools is erratic, uncertain, and undependable. While direct mandates may be communicated in some arenas of work, other arenas will have no guidelines or assistance interpreting expectations. Few coherent systems are in place: school-plan formats and decision-making processes vary, data are not gathered or formatted for school use, and resources can be found only for projects favored by district office personnel. Systematic accountability processes may be lacking at all levels, although some schools may have developed their own.

The absence of a coordinated district and school vision in Quadrant 2 districts results in program fragmentation. Though staff members may be involved in a variety of programs—athletics, instructional initiatives, community activities, the performing arts—there is a lack of coherence and focus. Because teachers often choose assignments without a substantive rationale, the most experienced among them end up with the highest achieving students, leaving beginning teachers with the neediest.

When someone has a great idea for professional development at a Quadrant 2 district, it will be organized and offered. The design of professional development days is usually left up to the schools, but may be unexpectedly vetoed or subverted by the district. District personnel will periodically scurry to pull things together in response to newspaper or Realtor accounts of school performance.

Quadrant 2 districts and many of their schools pride themselves on their individualism and entrepreneurial flare. Staff members at all levels who work from a systematic framework (such as the Leadership Capacity Matrix) will frequently be frustrated by the lack of follow-through and continuity throughout the district. There may only be one or two administrators in the district who can be looked to for consistent support.

Quality and student performance vary widely in Quadrant 2 district schools. Some schools do of course address student-performance issues creatively, but most stick to conventional, aggregated measures. In these latter schools, the more vulnerable students will fall through the cracks.

The Quadrant 2 district needs to develop a shared vision, accompanying structures, and follow-through strategies. The superintendent needs to either lead this effort or support those who can.

The Quadrant 3 District

Quadrant 3 district administrators and many of the teachers understand the direction in which the district is moving because it is framed by a vision, a strategic plan, and shared leadership structures at the school and district levels. Both the district and the school teams are developing internal accountability systems designed to use evidence to improve decisions and practice, and for which purpose a large degree of authority and many resources are decentralized. Professional development, though focused on the shared vision and goals, may still lack adequate follow-up in the form of practice, observation, and coaching. Student achievement and development are improving, however, and the gaps

between racial and socioeconomic student groups are narrowing.

The Quadrant 3 district has not yet "gone to scale" to achieve broad participation, which may be lacking among different groups for different reasons:

- Principals may be using shared decision-making structures in superficial ways;
- Teachers may still remain outside the decision-making circle, expressing resistance and failing to change classroom practice;
- Members of the professional associations may depend too much on adversarial bargaining; and
- Parents, the school board, and community members may continue to hold out for narrow agendas.

Processes within Quadrant 3 districts need to be made more inclusive and established throughout the district, which might need to introduce fewer initiatives and goals so that thoughtful conversations can deepen participation and commitment. In addition, staff members need to be coached as they expand their capabilities for democratic leadership.

The Quadrant 4 District

The Quadrant 4 district in which Belvedere Middle School resides has achieved broad and skillful participation in the work of leadership at all levels. Leadership is widely distributed among teachers, administrators, students, parents, and community members. A shared vision, which is continually reviewed and kept vibrant, results in program coherence. Inquiry-based accountability systems inform practice at all levels. Accountability is reciprocal as well, meaning that both the district and the schools seek constructive feedback from each other. Such reciprocity suggests high engagement with limited reliance on rules and regulations. Staff members are hired through a collaborative process within a framework that integrates district and school responsibilities for professional selection and development. Student achievement and development are either high or steadily improving among all schools in the district, regardless of student ethnicity, gender, or socioeconomic status.

The greatest challenge for the Quadrant 4 district—as with the Quadrant 4 school—is sustainability. As we will see in Chapter 10, sustainability involves the capacity to self-organize flexibly, the art of conversation, and the depth and breadth of leadership participation, enculturation, and pacing.

The Features of a Quadrant 4 District

The characteristics of Quadrant 4 districts as listed in the matrix in 9.1 are complementary, but not identical, to those in Quadrant 4 of the school matrix. These features recognize the dual nature of district leadership, which requires us to create a high leadership capacity district while simultaneously developing and supporting leadership capacity in schools; by performing the former, central administrators can model and facilitate the latter.

A learning organization exemplifies the definition of leadership offered in Chapter 1: reciprocal, purposeful learning in community. Organizational reciprocity—as opposed to a "loose" (decentralized) or "tight" (centralized) system—is "a dynamic of mutual responsibility characterized by shared vision, leadership, learning, expectations, and resources" (Lambert, 2001). Under such conditions, individuals and groups are simultaneously accountable.

LEADERSHIP CAPACITY FEATURE #1

District administrators and board members model, develop, and support broad-based, skillful participation in the work of leadership.

The classic organizational chart is an ancient artifact of hierarchical districts. It is usually designed to demonstrate lines of authority and reporting patterns, causing us to think of organizations strictly in terms of authority relationships rather than student learning outcomes.

The Cupertino School District, a diverse district of more than 15,000 students in the San Francisco Bay area, set about to change old patterns by developing the leadership capacity of the district. This work began with the creation of a new organizational graphic and gave rise to a new vision, mission, and strategic plan. The nucleus of the atom, represented by the center of the triangle, is student achievement and development supported by curriculum, instruction, and assessment. Superintendent Bill Bragg describes the new organizational chart (Figure 9.2):

> The key element of this model is that it is not linear, as is the case with most organizational charts. It suggests that conversations are occurring and decisions are being made in different areas or departments concurrently. All actions need to complement and build on one another in order for the organization to support students coherently and consistently . . . each action having student achievement and development at its core. It is equally important that each entity of the organization interact with the others in order to learn about their functions and natures. A common set of norms, behaviors, and expectations for leadership roles is critical. This model is not about control, but rather the enhancement of the district's central purpose through the most effective use of resources. There is a built-in interdependence resulting in mutual support and success.

Bragg reports that this graphic has changed the conversations, and the essential questions that drive them, by keeping their focus on student learning (personal communication, 2002).

Decisions in a Quadrant 4 school are made by interconnected school, cross-school, and

FIGURE 9.2
Cupertino Union School District Organizational Graphic

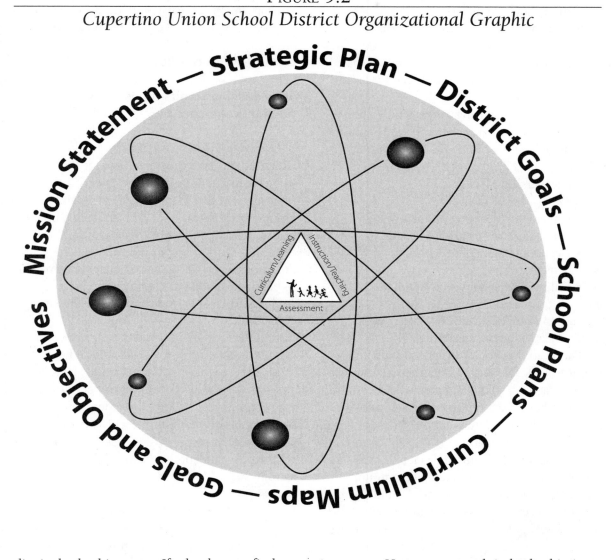

district leadership teams. If school teams find that student writing performance, for example, is less than adequate, cross-school or cluster teams will look for patterns in student writing among schools and present their findings to the district leadership team for discussion. The decision-making and inquiry processes at every school, in other words, are directly related to other schools and to the district.

Though the roles of superintendents and principals are changing, strong leadership is still important. However, strength in leadership is not to be confused with the tendency of Quadrant 1 leaders to rely heavily on directing, telling, and commanding. Instead, strong leadership behaviors might include the following:

- Insisting that the community convene around the development of a shared vision
- Framing essential instructional support with a standards emphasis, multiple assessments, and program coherence

- Requiring that democratic processes be used throughout the district
- Demanding that tough questions be raised and problems resolved together
- Allowing for solutions to arise out of shared dialogue and not necessarily preconceived outcomes
- Confronting and engaging political alliances that have existed in the outer circle of district influence

Strong leadership *is not*

- Unilaterally deciding on the one best curriculum or principal.
- Declaring a new policy without consultation.
- Selling a personal vision to others.

Figure 9.3 describes characteristics of superintendent leadership in greater detail.

Earlier in this book I discussed how important it is for leadership to be distributed widely among teachers, students, parents, and community members. Each of these leadership roles permeates district culture and provides for broad-based participation.

In Scottsbluff, Nebraska, leadership roles are widely distributed among school community members. Teachers, administrators, and board members receive leadership training that enables them to lead grade-level meetings, collaborative teams, book review groups, and board meetings. The district's Director of Curriculum and Technology Joe Baker captures the concept of leadership capacity:

> Leadership in a district and building does not happen by the chance of getting a strong superintendent or principal. Too often leadership lies in the hands of one person, and if that person leaves the boardroom or the superintendent's or principal's office, direction for the district is lost. By

becoming part of the culture of district leadership, and the capacity for it, the district will stay the course. (personal communication, 2001)

LEADERSHIP CAPACITY FEATURE #2

Shared vision results in districtwide program coherence.

A shared vision is the touchstone from which other district actions flow; for the vision to be meaningful, it should be created by representatives from all school community groups. Because they are derived from core values, school and district visions should be congruent if they are to guide action. This does not mean that the vision statements need to be identical, but they do need to be mediated so that participants understand how they are connected.

In order to ascertain whether our behaviors are consistent with our visions, and to keep those visions vibrant, program implementation and renewal should be subject to periodic dialogue and review. Will the program being considered enable you to implement your vision? If your school or district vision was alive and well, what would students and adults be doing and learning?

LEADERSHIP CAPACITY FEATURE #3

An inquiry-based accountability system informs decision making and practice at classroom, school, and district levels.

I agree with Linda Darling-Hammond (1993) when she defines accountability as the capacity of schools and districts to organize themselves so that students don't fall through the cracks, to create a means for continual collegial inquiry (i.e., posing hard questions in order for individuals and groups of students to succeed), and to

FIGURE 9.3
Acts of Superintendent Leadership

- Developing a shared vision of excellence about teaching, learning, and leading with students, adults, and the community—and resisting the temptation to make unilateral decisions that may be inconsistent with the vision
- Maintaining focus on the shared vision
- Establishing an infrastructure of democratic practices and structures that involve school community members in broad-based, skillful participation in the work of district leadership
- Articulating a range of best practices about human learning, avoiding "right" answers and one-size-fits-all solutions
- Cocreating accountability systems based on inquiry at all levels
- Translating policies, mandates, and requirements in ways that maintain the congruence between vision and practice
- Ensuring collaboration among multiple partners (e.g., among community agencies and alliances, universities, and other regional and state organizations)
- Developing transparent, multilayered communications systems
- Apprising community members of whom to talk with and how to get actions initiated
- Modeling actions that build system and individual leadership capacity
- Educating and engaging board members in understandings of board roles, vision, learning, resource management, and policy development
- Seeking and developing educators committed to the district vision, shared leadership, and active engagement in their own learning
- Securing essential resources, including finance, time, talent, and ideas

use authority responsibly to make the changes necessary.

An inquiry-based accountability system first and foremost requires us to pose questions, examine evidence of student learning, and engage in reflection, dialogue, and action. This process, often referred to as a "learning cycle," occurs internally within both schools and districts; the district and school processes are connected to each other by the practices of the decision-making team. This connection should be reciprocal: whereas the district is accountable to schools for services and resources, for instance, schools are accountable to the district and community for student performance.

LEADERSHIP CAPACITY FEATURE #4

Organizational relationships involve high district engagement and low bureaucratization.

High engagement means frequent interaction and two-way communication, problem solving instead of solution giving, mutual coordination and reciprocal influence, and some shared goals and objectives. Low bureaucratization means an absence of extensive rules and regulations (Louis, 1989; Lambert, 1998).

Policies and procedures should support engagement rather than bureaucratization. The Saratoga (California) School District, for example, uses a problem-resolution policy (Appendix F) to describe a high-engagement approach to problem solving for all community members. Participants solve their own problems rather than relying on solutions handed down by those in formal leadership positions, thus redistributing authority and responsibility for their actions. Policies that promote high engagement increase the possibility of sustainable improvement.

Contracts with professional organizations are often sources of bureaucratization: those that limit faculty meeting times, peer observation, scheduling, and the time frame of the working day and year can constrict a school's capacity to improve. More collegial forms of negotiations can realign district relationships so that all parties are working together to improve student learning. The practice of interest-based bargaining, for instance, allows administrators and teachers to meet face-to-face in a collaborative, open approach to identify shared goals and interests. With these shared goals as a foundation, participants are able to hold respectful conversations characterized by skillful dialogue and listening. Such forms of bargaining can ultimately change the working conditions for teachers.

Charter schools and districts have the as-yet-unrealized potential to minimize regulations in order to experiment with new ideas. In this book, we have seen how Sherman Oaks Charter School and Hickman Community Charter District successfully expanded the boundaries of schooling and engaged partners deeply in that process.

Communication processes that are open, personal, and reciprocal ensure high engagement.

When district staff members serve on school or cluster teams, few secrets exist, and everybody learns new information at the same time, so trusting relationships can flourish. Many districts have "shadow governments" that make decisions behind the scenes of the district's public persona. Although confidentiality in personnel matters may be appropriate, most secrets are best reserved for romance novels.

High engagement can inform an assessment of practice, during which we might ask whether the practice in question will

- Encourage parents and community members to become involved,
- Potentially alienate any group, and
- Help all involved to build trusting relationships.

LEADERSHIP CAPACITY FEATURE #5

Professional selection and development recruits and educates learners and leaders.

Selection of New Personnel

When selecting new personnel, look for the following dispositions and perspectives to ensure that candidates are compatible with the quest for high leadership capacity:

- A willingness to participate in decision making
- A constructivist philosophy of learning (though the candidates may not use the term)
- A sense of responsibility for all of the students in the school
- A readiness to work together to accomplish the school's goals
- An understanding of how to improve one's craft

Naturally, before the final selection is made, district and school expectations need to be clarified for the candidate.

The succession of the principal plays a large role in a school's continuing success. School and district personnel should collaborate to select principals based on school-generated criteria. Too often, districts unilaterally assign a principal who is unsuited for the school's level of development. I am increasingly persuaded that selecting a principal from among the teacher leaders in a Quadrant 3 or 4 school is a good idea.

The Professional Development of Educational Leaders

Professional development in a district should be seen as an opportunity to learn by constructing meaning and knowledge together. Such learning occurs in skillful conversations with each other in teams, coaching pairs, faculty meeting dialogues and so on.

In the Berryessa (California) Union School District, cross-school collaborative action teams engage in learning cycles and base their discussions on the assumption that every student has the right to

- Be held to high expectations and standards
- Access the latest technology in the learning environment
- Expect the highest quality of thinking and behavior from the staff
- Experience effective and appropriate instruction
- Feel safe and secure
- Be heard and understood

Team representatives lead learning cycles at their own sites by convening grade-level meetings, planning professional development days, and reviewing data to set goals for student achievement (Speck & Knipe, 2001).

In San Leandro, California, principals and the superintendent created a mentoring program for new principals. Under the program, principals with at least three years experience work one-on-one with new principals during a summer workshop and throughout the year to discuss school plans and district programs and troubleshoot any issues that arise. Strong district involvement ensures that all new principals are more likely to be served well.

When the Northern Lights School District in Alberta, Canada, began its journey toward capacity-building professional development, little time, few resources, and negligible energy were devoted to adult learning. Superintendent Ed Wittchen, a powerful advocate for professional development, crafted a major shift in the district's thinking by declaring that all educators were leaders, that resources invested in educators were resources invested in children, and that learning occurs in many settings, inside and outside of the system. Consequently, educators in the Northern Lights system benefit from 90-minute blocks of learning time every other week and leadership development programs at the district, university, national, and international levels (along with follow-up study groups). Any new findings are shared in teams throughout the system. When districts and schools coordinate focused professional development, everyone benefits from the expanded opportunities for adult learning and increased competence and confidence.

Districts clearly play a unique role in professional development—after all, schools cannot ensure consistent quality for all of the district's students on their own. The broader perspective, greater resources, and more extensive connections of the district should encourage administrators to

- Keep the vision of student learning on the planning table at all times

- Convene and sustain professional conversations
- Connect professional development to inquiry-based accountability
- Develop districtwide mentoring, coaching, and teacher support programs
- Coordinate school- and district-initiated professional development so that schools can maximize their collaborative learning and the district can bring all its schools together around large issues
- Secure a balance between internal and external learning opportunities through regional academies, networks, and universities
- Provide support, time, and resources and coordinate calendars for professional development

Leadership Capacity Feature #6

Student achievement and development is either high or steadily improving among all schools, with equitable outcomes for all students.

In Chapter 6, I discussed instructional practices that contribute to the development of student learning and leading. Professional development is particularly important in student learning because it shapes teacher beliefs, assumptions, and practice. The district should assume its responsibility as keeper of the vision and

- Develop policies that prohibit inequitable access, opportunities, and outcomes for students (e.g., tracking; short-term fixes with problematic long-term results, such as scripted reading; and too narrow a curriculum focused only on basic skills)
- Assist in the creation of small schools, or of communities within schools

- Develop staffing patterns that allow for comprehensive guidance programs and "looping" in order to develop long-term relationships.
- Create assessment policies that provide for multiple measures rather than relying solely on standardized test scores, and help format data so that it is accessible and sensible
- Make time and support available for parents and students

Conclusion

As you read this chapter, you may wonder whether it isn't contradictory of me to suggest that rules and regulations be kept at a minimum while simultaneously recommending multiple guidelines for district action. Fair point: I do indeed recommend that we generally eschew rules that are aimed at individual behaviors or that restrict risk taking and innovation. The guidelines that I suggest here are "enablers"— they serve to facilitate behaviors and actions that develop leadership capacity. Remember, leadership capacity is content-free—for example, it doesn't promote certain math programs over others—but it is not value-free. The suggestions offered here, therefore, are designed to lead us toward the values acquired in the higher stages of human development: equity, social justice, and caring.

Questions and Activities

1. If your district does not have a shared vision, begin the process now. If you do have a vision but haven't reviewed it in a while, place it on your team agenda to discuss whether it's still alive and well.

2. In a team meeting, assess your district using Figure 9.1 (the District Leadership Capacity Matrix). Identify and discuss areas for possible intervention.

3. Review Figure 9.3 (Acts of Superintendent Leadership). Add other acts that you consider important to the list. Place a plus sign beside actions that you do well and a question mark beside those you would like to improve or implement. Create a personal action plan for developing stronger capacity-building skills.

4. In a team that includes principals, post large pieces of chart paper on the wall and sketch an image of district decision-making groups, drawing lines to show how they connect. Discuss whether the teams are congruent, democratic, and inquiry-based.

5. How do you define accountability? Discuss with your team. Review the feature on inquiry-based accountability in this chapter and compare with your findings. Plan to improve your accountability processes.

6. In a conversation with parents and school board and community members, conduct a study of instructional effectiveness by considering the guiding actions listed under "Leadership Capacity Feature #6" in this chapter. Develop criteria for improving engagement and participation.

7. With district staff, design an evaluation of your professional development program and use it to assess district and school personnel. Include conversations at sites in the assessment process. Compile your findings, disseminate them to all, and plan for improvements.

8. Meet with a trusted colleague in the privacy of your office to examine how strongly you believe in equitable outcomes for all students. Do your policies and practices reveal that commitment?

CHAPTER 10
Sustaining Leadership Capacity

Two schools have had a major influence on my personal experiences of school leadership, and therefore my thinking about leadership capacity: Bell Junior High School in Golden, Colorado, and San Jose Middle School in Novato, California. I taught at Bell during the 1970–71 school year, just before moving to California. Bell was based on strong teacher leadership and the principles of open communication, problem solving, shared decision making, and accountability. It worked well for everyone in the school community.

A decade later, from 1980 to 1984, I was principal of San Jose Middle School. Since 1984, every principal and assistant principal at San Jose has been chosen from among the teacher leaders within the school. One assistant principal became principal and then superintendent, and other teacher leaders became district administrators.

Since leaving San Jose, I have deepened my understanding of (and sharpened my questions about) leadership capacity through experiences at the school, district, county, regional, and international levels. No question lingers more vividly in my imagination than, "How do we bring about sustainable school improvement?"

Jennifer's View of Sustainability

In Chapter 1, I noted that the district superintendent asked Jennifer how she would work with others to sustain high leadership capacity at Belvedere Middle School. This is how Jennifer replied:

> The major aim of leadership capacity development is sustained school improvement. Focused, professional conversation about student learning

is the primary catalyst for improving schools, but it's not enough. Also necessary are an understanding of participation (i.e., leadership as expressed by teachers, administrators, students, parents, and community members), collaborative roles and collective responsibilities, and reflection and inquiry; a passionate commitment to student learning; and outrage at unsatisfactory student achievement. I believe that I have the knowledge and skills necessary to lead this continuing journey with others. There will be uncertainties, surprises, and setbacks, to be sure, but I firmly believe we can weather them. As long as we keep the big picture in mind and commit to each other, our improvements will be sustained.

What Jennifer Learned About Sustainability

Jennifer's acknowledgment of uncertainty and the need for flexibility is perhaps the deepest insight she has garnered about leadership to date. If a school's capacity is built entirely on relationships, the fabric may be too soft or fluid unless the necessary structures are present. If, on the other hand, the essential structures—such as governance, teams, learning cycles, shared decision-making models, and accountability processes—are too rigid, they can become brittle and break under pressure. Because social systems are uncertain by their very nature, schools are fragile places.

Besides solid relationships and flexible structures, the development of leadership requires adults to practice synergy and self-organization. If relationships enable us to care, trust, and risk, structures are the media through which we do so. When we interact, synergy gives us the will to succeed together ("we have the capacity and the determination to make it happen"), and self-organization provides us with alternative means to success ("given the new challenges, let's reorganize ourselves in another way").

Jennifer found that engagement leads to synergy, which taps into our imaginations and allows us to visualize possible organizational changes. The process might be depicted like this:

Engagement → Synergy → Self-Organization

Because of this causal relationship, Jennifer learned to stay in the conversation even if the going was rough at first. When self-organization is achieved, you will notice that

- Completing the work necessary to achieve goals is more important than the length of a meeting;
- If there is more work to be done when a meeting adjourns, a teacher will suggest another time to get together;
- The principal doesn't need to convene all meetings;
- Many people participate in the discussion;
- Participants ask one another challenging questions;
- The energy levels of all involved rise; and
- Teachers, students, and parents initiate new ways of accomplishing the school's aims.

In Chapters 8 and 9, I described the Clayton, Missouri, experiment in self-organization. The district allowed teachers the discretion to plan their own learning, as long as the plans were aligned with district goals; the teachers answered by forming 35 district goal–centered study teams. As long as self-organization is accompanied by responsibility and authority, schools will sustain momentum and shared commitment.

Conditions for Sustainability

Senge and colleagues (1999) describe sustainability as a function of shared vision and personal mastery, team learning, and systems thinking (pp. 530–534). Each of these ideas is central to the work of leadership capacity—especially the fact that the critical features of such work are systemically interconnected. Other conditions for maintaining a school's capacity for leadership include

- A sustained sense of purpose,
- Succession planning and selection,
- Enculturation,
- A rhythm of development, and
- Conversion of practice into policy.

SUSTAINED SENSE OF PURPOSE

Sustaining a sense of purpose requires that we continually use the language of our school and district visions and that we formally revisit the vision at least once a quarter. It also means using the language of leadership capacity by asking questions about our work, such as the following:

- How are we doing with participation? Is anyone feeling left out?
- Are our skills sufficient? What else do we need to know?
- Are we hearing everybody's voices, and particularly those of students?
- How are our teams working?
- What evidence do we have that a given assumption is true?
- Who is responsible for what tasks?
- Are the student successes to date enough?
- What added value are we bringing to students' lives?

By focusing our questions in this manner, we turn the vision and conceptual framework of the school into daily touchstones that guide our professional conversations about student learning.

SUCCESSION PLANNING AND SELECTION

Succession planning and selection, which are characteristics of Quadrant 3 and 4 districts, requires that we select administrators who can

hit the road running and respect the school's purposes and progress. I recently met a university professor who was working with an urban Quadrant 1 school. The school's directive principal was retiring, which sounded like good news. The professor, however, was wary. "My fear is that the school staff and district will choose a principal just like the one who is leaving," he said. "They will seek to continue their current relationship with authority, which allows the staff to blame and avoid responsibility." This is a justifiable concern, and one of the reasons that Quadrant 1 and 2 schools need more district guidance in principal selection than Quadrant 3 and Quadrant 4 schools.

ENCULTURATION

Enculturation of new personnel enables new educators, parents, and students to enter midcourse and not feel alienated or confused. Such support—which should include orientation, mentoring, coaching, and the generous sharing of information and resources—increases the chances that the leadership culture will be seamless. Enculturation is everyone's responsibility.

RHYTHM OF DEVELOPMENT

A rhythm of development—a personal and collective ebb and flow—is necessary for staff members to sustain their energy. Even under the best conditions, some individuals burn out—not out of frustration and disappointment, necessarily, but out of exhaustion. By anticipating the possibility of burnout, school community members can intervene before they begin to feel a sense of failure for letting go of the process and outcomes. School community members need to orchestrate energy by

- Guarding against low-priority initiatives that draw attention away from the essential work of the school;

- "Gliding," during which time we consolidate and deepen our efforts;
- Rotating major responsibilities so that no one person carries a major task for too long;
- Letting individuals opt out of tasks occasionally when external or personal demands make it important to do so;
- Keeping reflection at the center of practice (remember that whenever you're tempted to cut reflection time because of other demands, it is actually time to increase it);
- Celebrating successes frequently; and
- Learning to occasionally say "no."

Your personal rhythm depends on context and begins with developing strategies to anticipate and address demands on your community.

PRACTICE AS POLICY

School practices last longer when they are enacted into policy. It is important, however, to distinguish between policies that facilitate the development of leadership capacity and those that compound bureaucratization. See Appendix F for a good example of the former.

Conclusion

The superintendent of Jennifer's district was intrigued and satisfied by what he had learned from Jennifer about her leadership skills, the leadership capacity of the school, and the principles of sustainability. After their conversation, he launched the process for selecting the new principal of Belvedere. The process was democratic, with broad participation from the school community. As we learned in Chapter 5, Jennifer ultimately got the job. She doesn't plan to leave anytime soon.

The work of leadership is characterized by several interdependent features. Involving teach-ers, administrators, students, parents, and community members in skillful ways promotes collective commitment to learning for all students. Launching such a shared and visionary journey into school improvement unites us as travelers on the journey toward school improvement that is challenging and deeply satisfying, and which leads to remarkable results for all learners. My hope is that this book has demystified the prospects of such a journey.

Questions and Activities

1. In small groups or teams in a staff meeting, ask participants to sincerely state how well they believe they are attending to their energy levels. As a whole group, discuss what you are doing to help each other sustain energy as well as what is draining you of it. Brainstorm strategies for addressing this ever-present issue.

2. When interviewing people new to the school (students included), leadership-team members can ask whether newcomers feel supported by the school community and, if so, what in particular has made them feel that way.

3. In a staff meeting, conduct a dialogue on the meaning of self-organization. Discuss in pairs to ensure a shared understanding of the concept. Ask the entire group: "What evidence is there that we are self-organizing? What additional evidence would we like to see?"

4. Celebrate your successes often. At the beginning of each staff meeting, have everyone state in a quick-write what they specifically and the school in general are doing especially well.

5. In a staff meeting, ask how well the school is developing and sustaining leadership capacity. Hand out the results of old surveys or assessment questions (see Chapter 3) as a reminder of where you used to be. Discuss in small groups, then in the whole group. What else needs to be done?

Leadership Capacity Strategies

Add your own strategies to each quadrant below.

Quadrant 1: Developing Reciprocal Relationships Possible strategies include: • Establishing collaborative norms • Solving problems • Using evidence in discussions • Coaching • • •	**Quadrant 2: Creating a Shared Purpose** Possible strategies include: • Finding shared values • Engaging in schoolwide collaborative action research • Running effective staff meetings • • •
Quadrant 3: Going to Scale Possible strategies include: • Involving everyone in schoolwide investigations and conversations • Using dialogue consistently • Learning conflict-resolution skills • • •	**Quadrant 4: Sustainability** Possible strategies include: • Revisiting the shared vision regularly • Creating multiple means of participation • Attending to succession planning • • •

APPENDIX B
Rubric of Emerging Teacher Leadership

Dependent	Independent	Interdependent	Leadership
A. Adult Development			
Defines self in relation to others in the community. Considers the opinions of others, particularly those in authority, to be highly important.	Defines self as independent from the group, separating personal needs and goals from those of others. Does not often see the need for group action.	Defines self as interdependent with others in the school community, seeking feedback and counsel from others.	Engages colleagues in acting out of a sense of self and shared values, forming interdependent learning communities.
Does not yet recognize the need for self-reflection. Tends to implement strategies as learned without making adjustments after reflective practice.	Engages in personal reflection leading to refinement of strategies and routines. Does not often share reflections with others. Focuses on argument for own ideas. Does not support systems designed to enhance reflective practice.	Engages in personal reflection to improve practice. Models improvements for others in the school community. Shares views with others and develops an understanding of others' assumptions.	Evokes reflection in others. Develops and supports a culture of self-reflection that may include collaborative planning, peer coaching, action research, and reflective writing.

From			To
Dependent	**Independent**	**Interdependent**	**Leadership**

A. Adult Development (cont.)

Dependent	Independent	Interdependent	Leadership
Does not regularly evaluate practice or systematically connect teacher and student behaviors.	Does not share results of self-evaluation with others, but typically ascribes responsibility for problems or errors to others, such as students or family.	Engages in self-evaluation and is highly introspective. Accepts shared responsibility as a natural part of the school community. Does not blame others when things go wrong.	Enables others to engage in self-evaluation and introspection, leading toward greater individual and shared responsibility.
Needs effective strategies to demonstrate respect and concern for others. Though polite, focuses primarily on own needs.	Shows respect toward others in most situations, usually in private. Can be disrespectful in public debates. Provides little feedback to others.	Consistently shows respect and concern for all members of the school community. Validates the qualities and opinions of others.	Encourages others to become respectful, caring, and trusted members of the school community. Recognizes that the ideas and achievements of colleagues are part of an overall goal of collegial empowerment.

B. Dialogue

Dependent	Independent	Interdependent	Leadership
Interacts with others primarily on a social level, and does not discuss common goals or group learning.	Discusses logistical issues and problems with others. Sees goals as individually set for each classroom; does not actively focus on common goals.	Communicates well with individuals and groups in the community as a means to create and sustain relationships and focus on teaching and learning. Actively participates in dialogue.	Facilitates effective dialogue among members of the school community in order to build relationships and focus the dialogue on teaching and learning.
Does not pose questions of or seek to influence the group. Participation is limited to consent or compliance.	Makes personal points of view explicit. When opposed to ideas, asks impeding questions that can derail the dialogue.	Asks questions and provides insights that reflect an understanding of the need to surface assumptions and address the goals of the community.	Facilitates communication among colleagues by asking provocative questions that lead to productive dialogue.

(continued)

From ——————————————————————————————————————→ To

Dependent	Independent	Interdependent	Leadership
B. Dialogue (cont.)			
Does not actively seek information or new professional knowledge that challenges current practices. Shares knowledge with others only when requested.	Attends staff development activities that are planned by the school or district. Occasionally shares knowledge during formal and informal gatherings. Does not seek knowledge that challenges status quo.	Studies own practice. Knows the most current information about teaching and learning, and uses it to alter teaching practices.	Works with others to construct knowledge through multiple forms of inquiry, action research, examination of disaggregated school data, and insights from others and from the outside research community.
Responds to situations in rote fashion and expects predictable responses from others. Is sometimes confused by variations from expected norms.	Responds to situations in different but predictable ways. Expects similar consistency from those in authority.	Responds to situations with open-mindedness and flexibility; welcomes the perspectives of others. Alters own assumptions during dialogue when evidence is persuasive.	Promotes open-mindedness and flexibility in others; invites multiple perspectives and interpretations to challenge old assumptions and frame new actions.
C. Collaboration			
Bases decision-making on personal wants and needs rather than those of the group as a whole.	Promotes individual autonomy in classroom decision-making. Relegates school decisions to the principal.	Actively participates in shared decision-making. Volunteers to follow through on group decisions.	Promotes collaborative decision-making that meets the diverse needs of the school community.
Sees little value in team building, but seeks team membership. Participates in teamwork but does not connect activities to larger school goals.	Does not participate in roles or settings that involve team building. Considers most team-building activities to be "touchy-feely" and frivolous.	Participates actively in team building; seeks roles and opportunities to contribute to the team. Sees teamwork as central to community.	Engages colleagues in team-building activities that develop mutual trust and promote collaborative decision-making.

(continued)

From ——————————————————————————————→ To			
Dependent	**Independent**	**Interdependent**	**Leadership**

C. Collaboration (cont.)

Dependent	Independent	Interdependent	Leadership
Either blames others or takes the blame personally for problems. Is uncertain about the specifics of his or her own involvement.	Plays the role of observer and critic; does not accept responsibility for emerging issues. Blames most problems on poor management.	Acknowledges that problems involve all members of the community. Defines problems and proposes approaches to address the situation. Does not consider assigning blame to be relevant.	Engages colleagues in identifying and acknowledging problems. Acts with others to frame problems and seek resolutions. Anticipates situations that may cause recurrent problems.
Refuses to recognize conflict in the school community. Misdirects frustrations into withdrawal or personal hurt. Avoids talking about issues that might evoke conflict.	Engages conflict as a means to surface competing ideas and approaches. Understands that conflict intimidates many.	Anticipates and seeks to resolve conflicts. Actively tries to channel conflicts into problem-solving endeavors. Is not intimidated by conflict, but does not seek it.	Surfaces, addresses, and mediates conflict within the school and with parents and community. Understands that negotiating conflict is necessary for personal and school change.

D. Organizational Change

Dependent	Independent	Interdependent	Leadership
Focuses on present situations and issues; seldom plans for the future. Expects certainty.	Demonstrates forward thinking for own classroom. Does not usually connect personal planning to the future of the school.	Develops forward-thinking skills for working with others and planning for school improvements. Bases future goals based on common values and vision.	Provides for and creates opportunities to engage others in visionary thinking and planning based on common core values.
Maintains a low profile during school change, and does not get involved with group processes. Tries to comply with changes, and expects compliance from others.	Questions the status quo; suggests that others need to change in order to improve it. Selects changes that reflect a personal philosophy. Opposes or ignores practices that require a schoolwide focus.	Is enthusiastic and actively involved in school change. Leads by example. Explores possibilities and implements changes for both personal and professional development.	Initiates innovative change; motivates and draws others into the action for school and district improvements. Encourages others to implement practices that support schoolwide learning. Provides follow-up planning and coaching support.

(continued)

From ──► To

Dependent	Independent	Interdependent	Leadership
D. Organizational Change (cont.)			
Is culturally unaware and naive about the sociopolitical implications of racial, cultural, and gender issues. Treats everybody the same regardless of background.	Is becoming more sensitive to the political implications of diversity. Acknowledges that cultural differences exist and influence individuals and organizations.	Appreciates own cultural identity and the cultural differences of others. Applies this understanding in the classroom and school.	Is committed to the value of cultural differences and builds on those values. Actively seeks to involve others in designing programs and policies that support a multicultural world.
Attends to students in own classroom. Is possessive of children and space; has not yet secured a developmental view of children.	Exhibits concern for the level of preparation of students and their readiness to meet established standards.	Is concerned for all children in the school (not just those in own classroom) and their future educational performances.	Works with colleagues to develop programs and policies that take holistic view of child development (e.g., multigrade classrooms, multiyear teacher assignments, parent education, follow-up studies).
Is cordial when working alongside new teachers, but does not offer assistance. Lacks the confidence to provide others with feedback.	Limits information shared with new teachers to that dealing with administrative functions (e.g., attendance accounting, grade reports). Does not offer to serve as a master teacher.	Collaborates with, supports, and gives feedback to new and student teachers. Often serves as master teacher.	Takes responsibility for the support and development of systems for new and student teachers. Develops collaborative programs among schools, districts, and universities.
Displays little interest in the selection of new teachers; assumes they will be appointed by the district or by others in authority.	Assumes that the district will recruit and appoint teachers. Has not proposed a more active role to the teachers' association.	Is actively involved in setting the criteria for and selecting new teachers.	Advocates the development of hiring practices that involve teachers, parents, and students in the schools, district, and teachers' associations; promotes the hiring of diversity candidates.

Continuum of Emerging Teacher Leadership

A. Adult Development

Defines self as interdependent with others in the school community, seeking feedback and counsel from others.

$\longrightarrow$ Engages colleagues in acting out of a sense of self and shared values, forming interdependent learning communities.

Engages in personal reflection to improve practice. Models improvements for others in the school community. Shares views with others and develops an understanding of others' assumptions.

$\longrightarrow$ Evokes reflection in others. Develops and supports a culture of self-reflection that may include collaborative planning, peer coaching, action research, and reflective writing.

Engages in self-evaluation and is highly introspective. Accepts shared responsibility as a natural part of the school community. Does not blame others when things go wrong.

$\longrightarrow$ Enables others to engage in self-evaluation and introspection, leading toward greater individual and shared responsibility.

Consistently shows respect and concern for all members of the school community. Validates the qualities and opinions of others.

$\longrightarrow$ Encourages others to become respectful, caring, and trusted members of the school community. Recognizes that the ideas and achievements of colleagues are part of an overall goal of collegial empowerment.

B. Dialogue

Communicates well with individuals and groups in the community as a means to create and sustain relationships and focus on teaching and learning. Actively participates in dialogue.

$\longrightarrow$ Facilitates effective dialogue among members of the school community in order to build relationships and focus the dialogue on teaching and learning.

Asks questions and provides insights that reflect an understanding of the need to surface assumptions and address the goals of the community.

$\longrightarrow$ Facilitates communication among colleagues by asking provocative questions that lead to productive dialogue.

(continued)

B. Dialogue (cont.)

Studies own practice. Knows the most current information about teaching and learning, and uses it to alter teaching practices. → Works with others to construct knowledge through multiple forms of inquiry, action research, examination of disaggregated school data, and insights from others and from the outside research community.

Responds to situations with open-mindedness and flexibility; welcomes the perspectives of others. Alters own assumptions during dialogue when evidence is persuasive. → Promotes open-mindedness and flexibility in others; invites multiple perspectives and interpretations to challenge old assumptions and frame new actions.

C. Collaboration

Actively participates in shared decision making. Volunteers to follow through on group decisions. → Promotes collaborative decision making that meets the diverse needs of the school community.

Participates actively in team building; seeks roles and opportunities to contribute to the team. Sees teamwork as central to community. → Engages colleagues in team-building activities that develop mutual trust and promote collaborative decision making.

Acknowledges that problems involve all members of the community. Defines problems and proposes approaches to address the situation. Does not consider assigning blame to be relevant. → Engages colleagues in identifying and acknowledging problems. Acts with others to frame problems and seek resolutions. Anticipates situations that may cause recurrent problems.

Anticipates and seeks to resolve conflicts. Actively tries to channel conflicts into problem-solving endeavors. Is not intimidated by conflict, but does not seek it. → Surfaces, addresses, and mediates conflict within the school and with parents and community. Understands that negotiating conflict is necessary for personal and school change.

D. Organizational Change

Develops forward-thinking skills for working with others and planning for school improvements. Bases future goals on common values and vision. → Provides for and creates opportunities to engage others in visionary thinking and planning based on common core values.

D. Organizational Change (cont.)

Is enthusiastic and actively involved in school change. Leads by example. Explores possibilities and implements changes for both personal and professional development. ⟶ Initiates innovative change; motivates and draws others into the action for school and district improvements. Encourages others to implement practices that support schoolwide learning. Provides follow-up planning and coaching support.

Appreciates own cultural identity and the cultural differences of others. Applies this understanding in the classroom and school. ⟶ Is committed to the value of cultural differences and builds on those values. Actively seeks to involve others in designing programs and policies that support a multicultural world.

Is concerned for all children in the school (not just those in own classroom) and their future educational performances. ⟶ Works with colleagues to develop programs and policies that take holistic view of child development (e.g., multigrade classrooms, multiyear teacher assignments, parent education, follow-up studies).

Collaborates with, supports, and gives feedback to new and student teachers. Often serves as master teacher. ⟶ Takes responsibility for the support and development of systems for new and student teachers. Develops collaborative programs between schools, districts, and universities.

Is actively involved in setting the criteria for and selecting new teachers. ⟶ Advocates the development of hiring practices that involve teachers, parents, and students to the schools, district, and teachers' associations; promotes the hiring of diversity candidates.

APPENDIX D
Leadership Capacity Staff Survey

This form provides an assessment of the dispositions, knowledge, and skills needed to build leadership capacity in schools and organizations. It may be completed by a school staff member or by a colleague who is familiar with the work of that staff member; the form works best if is first completed by each staff member as a self-assessment, and then by two colleagues as further assessment of the same individual. The items are clustered according to the characteristics of Quadrant 4 schools. The scale to the right of each item can be translated thusly:

NO = not observed	CP = consistently performed
IP = infrequently performed	CTO = can teach to others
FP = frequently performed	

Please circle the rating for each item and add up the number of circled ratings in each column.

A. Broad-based participation in the work of leadership
(principals, teachers, students, parents, community members)

1. Assists in the establishment of representative governance and work groups (e.g., teams, councils, study groups)   NO   IP   FP   CP   CTO
2. Seeks to increase interactions among staff, students, and community members in order to build relationships and increase participation.   NO   IP   FP   CP   CTO
3. Shares authority and resources broadly.   NO   IP   FP   CP   CTO
4. Engages others in leading opportunities.   NO   IP   FP   CP   CTO

Total numbers   ___   ___   ___   ___   ___

B. Skillful participation in the work of leadership

Models, describes, and demonstrates the following skills:

a. Developing a shared vision with colleagues	NO	IP	FP	CP	CTO
b. Facilitating group processes	NO	IP	FP	CP	CTO
c. Communicating (especially listening and questioning)	NO	IP	FP	CP	CTO
d. Reflecting on practice	NO	IP	FP	CP	CTO
e. Inquiring into the questions and issues confronting the school community and using evidence to improve practice	NO	IP	FP	CP	CTO
f. Collaborating on planning	NO	IP	FP	CP	CTO
g. Challenging colleagues' beliefs and assumptions about who can lead and learn (as appropriate)	NO	IP	FP	CP	CTO
h. Managing conflict among adults	NO	IP	FP	CP	CTO
i. Problem-solving with colleagues, students, and parents	NO	IP	FP	CP	CTO
j. Managing change and transitions	NO	IP	FP	CP	CTO
k. Using active learning designs with adults	NO	IP	FP	CP	CTO
l. Communicating the relationship between leadership and learning	NO	IP	FP	CP	CTO

Total numbers   ___ ___ ___ ___ ___

C. Shared vision results in program coherence

1. Participates with others in the development of a shared vision and insists upon a vision that serves all children well.	NO	IP	FP	CP	CTO
2. Asks questions that keep the school on track with its vision.	NO	IP	FP	CP	CTO
3. Thinks about and aligns school standards, instruction, assessment, and programs according to the school's vision.	NO	IP	FP	CP	CTO
4. Suggests that the school keep its vision alive by reviewing it regularly.	NO	IP	FP	CP	CTO

Total numbers   ___ ___ ___ ___ ___

D. Inquiry-based use of information informs decisions and practice

1. Engages with others in posing questions about the work of the school.	NO	IP	FP	CP	CTO
2. Discovers and interprets classroom and school data.	NO	IP	FP	CP	CTO
3. Communicates with others about evidence.	NO	IP	FP	CP	CTO
4. Helps to create time for dialogue and reflection.	NO	IP	FP	CP	CTO
5. Uses evidence in decision-making processes.	NO	IP	FP	CP	CTO

Total numbers   ___ ___ ___ ___ ___

E. Roles and action reflect broad involvement, collaboration, and collective responsibility

1. Gives attention to the classroom, the school, the community, and the profession.	NO	IP	FP	CP	CTO
2. Encourages others to give attention to collegial activities beyond the classroom.	NO	IP	FP	CP	CTO
3. Attends to building relationships with others.	NO	IP	FP	CP	CTO
4. Encourages colleagues and parents to share responsibility for school improvement.	NO	IP	FP	CP	CTO
Total numbers	—	—	—	—	—

F. Reflective practice consistently leads to innovation

1. Encourages reflection among colleagues and students.	NO	IP	FP	CP	CTO
2. Uses reflective practices such as peer coaching, journal writing, collaborative planning.	NO	IP	FP	CP	CTO
3. Demonstrates and encourages initiative (e.g., posing questions, accessing resources, joining networks).	NO	IP	FP	CP	CTO
4. Invites and supports new ways of doing things.	NO	IP	FP	CP	CTO
5. Works with others to develop accountability criteria and processes for our school.	NO	IP	FP	CP	CTO
Total numbers	—	—	—	—	—

G. High or steadily improving student achievement and development

1. Works with members of the school community to establish and implement student expectations and standards.	NO	IP	FP	CP	CTO
2. Teaches and assesses so that all children learn.	NO	IP	FP	CP	CTO
3. Provides feedback to children and families about student progress.	NO	IP	FP	CP	CTO
4. Talks with families about learning expectations and performance.	NO	IP	FP	CP	CTO
5. Performs many roles as teacher/administrator of student learning: facilitator, coach, advisor, mentor.	NO	IP	FP	CP	CTO
6. Makes sure that school inquiry process includes evidence of student performance and development.	NO	IP	FP	CP	CTO
Total numbers	—	—	—	—	—

Scoring: Tally the number of responses in each category and note the responses in the columns below (NO/IP, FP/CP, and CTO).

	NO/IP	FP/CP	CTO
Broad-based participation in the work of leadership			
Skillful participation in the work of leadership			
Shared vision results in program coherence			
Inquiry-based use of information informs decisions and practice			
Roles and action reflect broad involvement, collaboration, and collective responsibility			
Reflective practice consistently leads to innovation			
High or steadily improving student achievement and development			

Suggestion: Identify specific dispositions and skills that fall into the NO/IP, FP/CP, or CTO categories. For skills in each category, do the following:

- NO/IP areas: Find opportunities to observe these skills in practice and be trained in them.
- FP/CP areas: Find more opportunities to demonstrate and practice these skills.
- CTO areas: Find opportunities to coach others and participate in formal governance groups.

Leadership Capacity School Survey

This school survey is designed to assess the leadership capacity of your school. The items are clustered according to the characteristics of Quadrant 4 schools. Once each staff member has completed the survey, the results can be presented in a chart depicting schoolwide needs. The numbers on the 1–5 scale represent the following:

> 1 = We do not do this at our school.
> 2 = We are starting to move in this direction.
> 3 = We are making good progress here.
> 4 = We have this condition well established.
> 5 = We are refining our practice in this area.

Circle the rating for each item and tally the score for each column first, then add the results for each column together and transfer the results to the scoring box on the last page.

A. Broad-based, skillful participation in the work of leadership.

In our school, we:

1. Have established representative governance groups	1	2	3	4	5
2. Perform collaborative work in large and small teams	1	2	3	4	5
3. Model leadership skills	1	2	3	4	5
4. Organize for maximum interaction among adults and children	1	2	3	4	5
5. Share authority and resources	1	2	3	4	5
6. Express our leadership by attending to the learning of the entire school community	1	2	3	4	5
7. Engage each other in opportunities to lead	1	2	3	4	5

Total (add circled numbers down and then across columns) _____ = __ __ __ __ __

B. **Shared vision results in program coherence.**

In our school, we:

1. Develop our school vision jointly	1	2	3	4	5
2. Ask each other questions that keep us on track with our vision	1	2	3	4	5
3. Think together about how to align our standards, instruction, assessment, and programs with our vision	1	2	3	4	5
4. Keep our vision alive by reviewing it regularly	1	2	3	4	5

Total (add circled numbers down and then across columns)   ____ = __ __ __ __ __

C. **Inquiry-based use of information to inform decisions and practice.**

In our school, we:

1. Use a learning cycle that involves reflection, dialogue, inquiry, and action	1	2	3	4	5
2. Make time available for this learning to occur (e.g., faculty meetings, ad hoc groups, teams)	1	2	3	4	5
3. Focus on student learning	1	2	3	4	5
4. Use data/evidence to inform our decisions and teaching practices	1	2	3	4	5
5. Have designed a comprehensive information system that keeps everyone informed and involved	1	2	3	4	5

Total (add circled numbers down and then across columns)   ____ = __ __ __ __ __

D. **Roles and actions reflect broad involvement, collaboration, and collective responsibility.**

In our school, we:

1. Have designed our roles to include attention to our classrooms, school, community, and profession	1	2	3	4	5
2. Seek to perform outside of traditional roles	1	2	3	4	5
3. Have developed new ways to work together	1	2	3	4	5
4. Have developed a plan for sharing responsibilities in the implementation of our decisions and agreements	1	2	3	4	5

Total (add circled numbers down and then across columns)   ____ = __ __ __ __ __

E. Reflective practice consistently leads to innovation.

In our school, we:

1. Make time for ongoing reflection (e.g., journaling, peer coaching, collaborative planning)   1   2   3   4   5
2. Encourage individual and group initiative by providing access to resources, personnel, and time   1   2   3   4   5
3. Have joined with networks of other schools and programs, both inside and outside the district, to secure feedback on our work   1   2   3   4   5
4. Practice and support new ways of doing things   1   2   3   4   5
5. Develop our own criteria for accountability regarding individual and shared work   1   2   3   4   5

Total (add circled numbers down and then across columns)   ____ = __ __ __ __ __

F. High or steadily improving student achievement and development

In our school, we:

1. Work with members of the school community to establish and implement expectations and standards   1   2   3   4   5
2. Teach and assess so that all children learn   1   2   3   4   5
3. Provide feedback to children and families about student progress   1   2   3   4   5
4. Talk with families about student performance and school programs   1   2   3   4   5
5. Have redesigned roles and structures to develop resiliency in children (e.g., teacher as coach/advisor/mentor, schoolwide guidance programs, community service)   1   2   3   4   5

Total (add circled numbers, down and then across columns)   ____ = __ __ __ __ __

Scoring: Add totals for each section. Possible scores can be found by multiplying the possible number of scores for each category by the number of staff completing the survey; the results for your particular school can be found by adding the actual scores of the staff completing the survey in each category (see the following table). Sections with the lowest scores are those in greatest need of attention. A score of 1 or 2 in the survey represents areas of greatest need, 3 and 4 represent strengths, and 5 represents exemplary work that reflects high leadership capacity. When you have completed the survey, discuss each section and identify possible areas for growth.

	Possible Scores	School Scores
Broad-based, skillful participation in the work of leadership	35 x ___=___	___
Shared vision results in program coherence	20 x ___=___	___
Inquiry-based use of information to inform decisions and practice	25 x ___=___	___
Roles and actions reflect broad involvement, collaboration, and collective responsibility	20 x ___=___	___
Reflective practice consistently leads to innovation	25 x ___=___	___
High or steadily improving student achievement and development	25 x ___=___	___

Problem Resolution Policy for the Saratoga Union School District

The Saratoga Union School District recognizes that parents, teachers, staff, and administrators share the purpose of educating students to their fullest potential, engaging their hearts and minds in learning, and that effective communication is an integral part of fulfilling that purpose. We further recognize that problems that are not resolved have a harmful effect on the learning community. Therefore, the Board of Trustees supports positive resolution of any concerns and encourages all parties involved to resolve these problems with the person(s) concerned. The procedures and process below are designed to accomplish this goal.

The Board of Trustees encourages positive, constructive suggestions that aid in our commitment to our purpose and vision.

Problem Resolution Procedure

Concerned parties are strongly encouraged to address issues of concern through the problem resolution process described below. It is assumed that parties enter this process in good faith and with a commitment to resolve, rather than prolong, the concern. The following pro-

Reprinted by permission.

cedures will enable the process to proceed successfully.

- Concerned school personnel shall respond to a call for an appointment as soon as possible, but at least within five working days.
- Conferences should be by appointment and at a time that will not interrupt professional or instructional activities.
- Participants in the process may include parents, students, staff, administrators and board members. Parents and teachers are encouraged to include students, as appropriate.
- The person bringing the problem to the attention of school or district personnel will be known as the "Initiator"; the school or district person to whom the problem is addressed will be known as the "Responder."
- Either the Initiator or the Responder may request (by mutual consent) that a third person, a mediator, be present to assist with the facilitation of the process.
- Training in the process will be provided to all members of the school community.
- If resolution is not obtained through the problem resolution process, appeal may be

made to 1) the Principal, 2) the Superintendent, 3) the School Board. At each appropriate level of appeal, the person(s) will solicit information from all involved and seek resolution. If the problem cannot be resolved at the Superintendent level and is referred to the Board, the Board's decision will be final.

- At no time during or after this process will actions by either party be construed as treating those concerned any differently[1] as a result of entering into the process.
- When hearing problems aired within the community, the members of the school community are encouraged to support and reinforce this policy. For instance, the community member may suggest that the Initiator seek resolution through the process.

Process to Resolve Problems

General responsibilities:

- Both parties may share the roles or agree that one participant will take the responsibility to facilitate and record the process.
- If at any time in the process either party feels uncomfortable or would like to think it over before participating, he or she may end the meeting. Reschedule as soon as possible.
- By mutual consent, a third party may be asked to attend a future meeting.

---

[1]For example, causing public embarrassment, discriminating against the person(s), or negatively affecting the standing of those concerned within their community of peers.

Steps	Initiator	Responder	Process Guidelines
1. Statement of the problem	States problem and identifies its perceived effects. Actively listens to the responder's view of same.	Actively listens to the initiator's view of the problem and its perceived effects. Identifies own view of same.	Both parties • Deliver first-person statements • Focus on the problem rather than the person • Illustrate points with examples • Actively listen and ask clarifying questions • Paraphrase unclear statements
2. Mutual exploration	Describes what a satisfactory solution might look like. Actively listens to the responder's articulation of same. Brainstorms solutions with responder, eliminating unacceptable ones and choosing the best.	Actively listens to the responder's description of what a satisfactory solution might look like. Articulates same. Brainstorms solutions with initiator, eliminating unacceptable ones and choosing the best.	Both parties • Generate as many solutions as possible without evaluating their appropriateness or effectiveness • Eliminate solutions that would not be effective or appropriate • Seek solutions that will meet shared or individual goals
3. Plan/ resolution	Develops a plan of action including steps, timeline (with a date for review), and responsibilities. Agrees with responder on distribution of notes.	Develops a plan of action including steps, timeline (with a date for review), and responsibilities. Agrees with initiator on distribution of notes.	Both parties • Choose a recorder • Decide whether notes should remain confidential or be shared with others

How Principals Build Leadership Capacity in Others

By Jeffrey Michael Pechura, "Head Learner" (principal) at Jefferson Elementary School in Wauwatosa, Wisconsin.

Note: *Jeff Pechura conducted a research study in three high leadership capacity schools in Wisconsin, one each in an urban, suburban, and rural setting (2001). The study closely examined principal behaviors that evoked leadership in others.*

As the demand for schools to improve student performance increases, the need for principals to cultivate broad-based, skillful participation in the work of leadership becomes essential. Principals who build and sustain leadership capacity share the following core beliefs:

1) Teachers, parents, and students can be successful leaders when given the opportunity to lead;

2) School community members must experience success in leadership roles;

3) Leadership capacity will be enhanced when the principal supports the leadership experiences of others;

4) Building the individual leadership capacity of the many builds organizational leadership capacity; and

5) The ability to do this important work lies within the school membership.

Figure AG.1 describes behaviors principals should engage in as they seek to build, develop, and sustain leadership capacity in others.

To begin building leadership capacity, a principal simply *talks* with teachers, parents, and students about taking on leadership roles and responsibilities. Once the dialogue begins, the principal *asks* others to participate, encourages involvement, and supports people as they engage in new leadership ventures. Teachers, parents, and students are eager to extend their leadership if and when asked to do so by the principal; he is the catalyst who must begin the conversations about sharing school leadership. When a principal is viewed as one who values shared leadership by talking about it with other school members and provides the necessary *help*

FIGURE AG.1
How Principals Build and Sustain Leadership Capacity

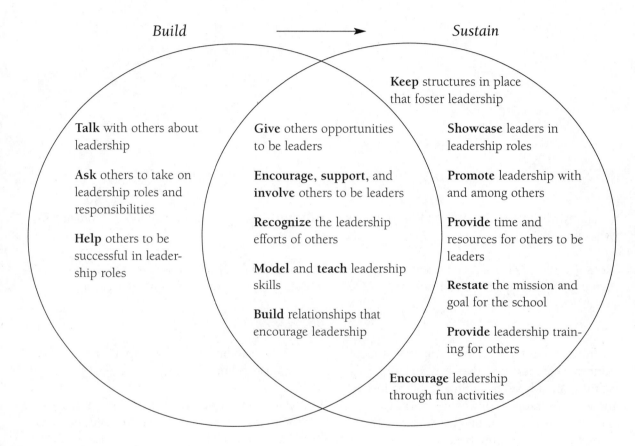

Build ⟶ *Sustain*

Keep structures in place that foster leadership

Talk with others about leadership

Ask others to take on leadership roles and responsibilities

Help others to be successful in leadership roles

Give others opportunities to be leaders

Encourage, support, and **involve** others to be leaders

Recognize the leadership efforts of others

Model and **teach** leadership skills

Build relationships that encourage leadership

Showcase leaders in leadership roles

Promote leadership with and among others

Provide time and resources for others to be leaders

Restate the mission and goal for the school

Provide leadership training for others

Encourage leadership through fun activities

for successful experiences, individual and collective leadership capacity begins to grow.

As a school moves toward becoming "leaderful" (Wheatley, 1992), the principal *balances the work of building and sustaining leadership capacity* at the same time. Different people are at different places on the leadership continuum. A principal's ability to *support, encourage, involve, recognize, model, teach,* and *give* others the opportunities to lead brings about the development of a *culture of leadership:* the continuous development and permeation of leadership and leaders within an

organization, making it live within the school community. A rural teacher explains:

> I think seeing the principal take on more leadership responsibilities encourages us to get involved, take on more leadership responsibilities, and fulfill the role as the leader we all are.

Support and encouragement can be accomplished through basic processes such as e-mail, written notes, verbal communication, recognition, and even body language. How a principal conveys support and encouragement is as important as what the principal communicates. When natural and positive, support and encouragement can make (rather than break) the development of leaders within a school.

The principal models, teaches, coaches, and provides leadership training to school staff members as they become skillful participants in leadership. When working as a leadership coach (see Chapter 3), the principal must be nonjudgmental and use strategies such as reflective listening, pausing, and critical questioning to help others become self-directed leaders. "Somehow, when we talk it through, I hear myself think," said one suburban teacher about her principal. "She asks me a couple of pointed questions . . . and the minute she asks me those questions, I get it."

A principal builds relationships and develops trust and rapport by treating others with respect. He admits mistakes, shares honestly, shows humility, listens and treats others professionally, thanks others for their leadership, and promotes leadership opportunities for the school membership fairly. Developing trust among teachers, parents, and students by maximizing personal interaction with them will decrease fear and anxiety in the organization and increase the opportunities for others to be leaders within the organization. In the words of one suburban principal, "trust begets trust."

How do principals sustain "leaderful" schools? They keep structures in place that foster leadership and showcase leaders in leadership roles (see Chapter 2). It is important to retain structures that promote leadership opportunities, such as a staff curriculum committee, parent advisory council, or student senate. Prin-

cipals also promote leadership within and among teachers, provide time and resources for teachers to be leaders, restate the mission and goals for the school, provide leadership training by allowing members of their school community to participate in leadership activities, and practice fun activities that contribute to sustaining leadership capacity (which itself helps to sustain the overall school culture). Every school principal owes it to the teachers, parents, and students he serves to expect that shared leadership be constantly and consistently exemplified by the school staff. As Barth (1990) so eloquently stated:

> School can be a place whose very mission is to ensure that everyone becomes a school leader in some ways and at some times in concert with others. A school can fulfill no higher purpose than to teach all of its members that they can make what they believe in happen and to encourage them to contribute to and benefit from the leadership of others. A community of leaders is a vision of what might become a vital part of the school culture. Without shared leadership, it is impossible for a shared culture to exist in a school. (pp. 171–172)

Principals use many simple yet effective strategies to build and sustain the leadership capacity of their school community. Principals, teachers, parents, and students realize the power and ability to develop a culture of leadership so that the work of teaching and learning continuously improves. Natural outcomes of a culture of leadership include ownership; collaboration; shared decision making; the development of a shared vision, mission, values, and goals; local action research; and interdependence.

References

Ackerman, R. H., Donaldson, G. A., Jr., & Van Der Bogert, R. (1996). *Making sense as a school leader.* San Francisco: Jossey-Bass Publishers.

Barkley, S. (Fall, 1999). Time: It's made, not found. *Journal of Staff Development.*

Barth, R. (1990). *Improving schools from within: Teachers, parents, and principals can make the difference.* San Francisco: Jossey-Bass Publishers.

Barth, R. (1999). *The teacher leader.* Providence, RI: The Rhode Island Foundation.

Boulay, A. (1999). [Untitled online article]. Available: http://www.opi-inc.com/margaret_wheatley.htm

California Professional Development Reform Initiative. (2000). *Finding time: Designs for learning.* Sacramento, CA: California Department of Education.

Canlas, R. (1996). *Conflict resolution: The effects of a comprehensive conflict resolution program on the safety of students in grades 4, 5, and 6 at Graham Elementary School in Newark, California, 1992–1996.* Hayward, CA: California State University, Hayward.

Caplan, R. (1999). *Beating the odds: Case studies of successful leadership leading to instances of powerful teaching and learning in the Oakland schools.* Unpublished master's thesis, California State University, Hayward, California.

Chan, Y. (February 17, 1999). *The little school that could.* San Mateo, CA: The California Professional Development Consortia.

Conzemius, A. (Fall, 1999). Ally in the office. *Journal of Staff Development, 20*(4), 31–34.

Conzemius, A., & O'Neill, J. (2001). *Building shared responsibility for student learning.* Alexandria, VA: Association for Supervision and Curriculum Development.

Costa, A., & Kallick, B. (Eds.). (2000). *Habits of mind: a developmental series.* Alexandria, VA: Association for Supervision and Curriculum Development.

Darling-Hammond, L. (1993). Reframing the school reform agenda: Developing capacity for school transformation. *Phi Delta Kappan, 76*(10), 752–761.

Developmental Studies Center. (1998). *The Child Development Project: A brief summary of the project and findings from three evaluation studies.* Oakland, CA: Author.

Garmston, R., & Wellman, B. (1999). *The adaptive school.* Norwood, MA: Christopher-Gordon.

Goleman, D. (1995). *Emotional intelligence.* New York: Bantam Books.

Goleman, D., Boyatzis, R., & McKee, A. (December, 2001). Primal leadership: The hidden driver of great performance. *Harvard Business Review.*

Hammond, Z. (October, 1999). *Equity research brief.* San Francisco: Bay Area School Reform Collaborative.

Haycock, K. (November, 2000). *Exceeding expectations.* San Mateo, CA: California Professional Development Consortia.

Haycock, K. (March, 2001). Closing the achievement gap. *Educational Leadership, 58*(6), 6–11.

Henderson, A. T., & Raimondo, B. N. (December 3, 2001). Unlocking parent potential: The online community for principals, assistant principals, and aspiring principals. Reston, VA: National Association of Secondary School Principals.

Keene, E. O., & Zimmerman, S. (1997). *Mosaic of thought: Teaching comprehension in a reader's workshop.* New York: Heinemann.

Kohm, B. (May, 2002). Open for discussion. *Educational leadership, 50*(8).

Kohn, A. (April, 1998). Only for my kid: How privileged parents undermine school reform. *Phi Delta Kappan.*

Kretzmann, J. P. (2001). "Ten commandments" for involving young people in community building. In N. Henderson, B. Bernard, & N. Sharp-Light (Eds.). *Mentoring for resiliency.* San Diego, CA: Resiliency in Action.

Krovetz, M. L. (1999). *Fostering resiliency.* Thousands Oaks, CA: Corwin Press.

Lambert, L. (1998). *Building leadership capacity in schools.* Alexandria, VA: Association for Supervision and Curriculum Development.

Lambert, L. (Fall, 2001). The petulant pendulum: The case for organizational reciprocity and the role of the superintendent. *Educational leadership and administration.*

Lambert, L., Walker, D., Zimmerman, D., Cooper, J., Gardner, M., Lambert, M. D., & Ford-Slack, P. J. (1995). *The constructivist leader.* New York: Teachers College Press.

Lambert, L., Walker, D., Zimmerman, D., Cooper, J., Gardner, M., Lambert, M. D., & Szabo, M. (2002). *The constructivist leader* (2nd ed.). New York: Teachers College Press.

Lambert, M. D., & Gardner, M. E. (2002). The school district as interdependent learning community. *The constructivist leader* (2nd ed.). New York: Teachers College Press.

Lewis, A. C. (March, 2002). School reform and professional development. *Phi Delta Kappan, 83*(7), 488.

Lieberman, A., & Wood, D. (2001). The work of the National Writing Project: Social practices in a network context. Palo Alto, CA: The Carnegie Foundation.

Lipton, L., & Wellman, B. (2001). *Mentoring matters: A practical guide to learning-focused relationships.* Sherman, CT: Miravia.

Louis, K. S. (1989). The role of the school district in school improvement. In M. Holmes, L. Leithwood, & D. Musella (Eds.), *Educational policy for effective schools* (145–167). Toronto: OISE Press.

Martinez, P. (January, 2001). *The UCLA School of Management program.* Address presented at the Association of California School Administrators' Superintendent's Symposium, Monterey, CA.

Meek, A. (February, 2002). The benefits of smallness. *Classroom leadership, 5*(5), 8.

National Education Commission on Time and Learning. (1994). *Prisoners of time.* Washington, DC: U.S. Government Printing Office.

Newmann, F. M., & Wehlage, G. G. (1995). *Successful school restructuring: A report of the public and educators by the Center on Organization and Restructuring of Schools.* Madison, WI: Center on Organization and Restructuring of Schools.

New Teachers Center. (1995). *California Standards for the Teaching Profession continuum.* Santa Cruz: University of California.

Olsen, L. (November, 2000). *Accountability to whom for what? Maintaining a focus on achievement and equity for all.* San Mateo, CA: California Professional Development Consortia.

Olson, L. (November 1, 2000). Principals try new styles as instructional leaders. *Education Week of the Web.*

Panasonic Foundation. (July, 1999). Learning and leading at all levels. *Strategies for School System Leaders on District Level Change, 6*(1), 8–10.

Pechura, J. (2001). *What principals do to build and sustain the leadership capacity of teachers, parents, and students in elementary schools.* Doctoral dissertation, Cardinal Stritch University, Milwaukee, Wisconsin.

Preece, A. (1997). Spreading the good word. In A. Costa & R. Liebmann (Eds.), *The process-centered school.* Thousand Oaks, CA: Corwin Press.

Reeves, D. B. (2000). *Accountability in action: A blueprint for learning organizations.* Denver, CO: Advanced Learning Press.

Reynolds, M. R. (2002). *Connecting with students (a personal assessment test).* Available: http://www.maryrobinsonreynolds.com/pages/semcolors.html

Schmoker, M. (1996). *Results: The key to continuous school improvement.* Alexandria, VA: Association for Supervision and Curriculum Development.

Schmoker, M. (Spring, 2002). Up and away. *Journal of Staff Development* [online], *23*(2), 1–8.

Senese, J. (1999). *The paradoxes of staff development.* Highland Park, IL: Highland Park High School.

Senge, P., Kleiner, A., Roberts, C., Ross, R., Roth, G., & Smith, B. (1999). *The dance of change: A fifth discipline resource.* New York: Doubleday.

Sparks, D. (Summer, 2000). An interview with Kati Haycock: Low incomes, high hurdles. *National Staff Development Council Journal, 21*(3), 37–40.

Speck, M., & Knipe, C. (2001). *Why can't we get it right?* Thousand Oaks, CA: Corwin.

Spillane, J., Halverson, R., & Diamond, J. (April, 2001). Investigating school leadership practice: A distributed perspective. *Research News and Comment.*

Van Linden & Fertman, C. (1998). *Youth leadership.* San Francisco: Jossey-Bass.

Von Oech, R. (1986). *A kick in the seat of the pants.* New York: Harper Row.

Walker, D. (2002). Constructivist leadership: Standards, equity, and learning—weaving whole cloth from multiple strands. In L. Lambert, D. Walker, D. Zimmerman, J. Cooper, M. Gardner, M. D. Lambert & M. Szabo (eds.), *The Constructivist Leader* (2nd ed.). New York: Teachers College Press.

Wasley, P. (2002). Small classes, small schools: The time is now. *Educational Leadership, 59*(5), 6–10.

Wheatley, M. (1992). *Leadership and the new science: Discovering order in a chaotic world.* San Francisco: Berrett-Koehler Publishers.

Wiggins, G., & McTighe, J. (1998). *Understanding by design.* Alexandria, VA: Association for Supervision and Curriculum Development.

Index

About the Author

Linda Lambert is professor emeritus at California State University, Hayward. She began her career in the field of probation, where she soon discovered that influencing education held more promise for influencing the lives of children. Since then, she has worked as a teacher leader, a principal, a district and county professional development director, the coordinator of a Principals' Center and Leadership Academy, the designer of four major restructuring programs, an international consultant, and a professor.

In the late 1980s and throughout the 1990s, Linda helped set up a National Curriculum Center in Egypt and worked in leadership development with thousands of principals, teachers, and district personnel in the United States, Canada, Mexico, Australia, and Thailand. She is the lead author of *The Constructivist Leader* (first and second editions, 1995 & 2002), *Who Will Save Our Schools: Teachers as Constructivist Leaders* (1997), author of *Building Leadership Capacity in Schools* (1998), and coauthor of *Developing Leadership Capacity for School Improvement* (2003), as well as of numerous articles and book chapters. Linda's research and consultancy interests include leadership, leadership capacity, professional and organizational development, and school and district restructuring.

Linda and her husband, Morgan, have five children, eleven grandchildren, and one great-grandchild. They alternate their residence between Oakland and The Sea Ranch, California. You may reach her by e-mail at Linlambert@aol.com, by phone at 510-569-8840, or by fax at 510-569-8858.

Related ASCD Resources

Books

Analytic Process for School Leaders by Cynthia T. Richetti and Benjamin B. Tregoe (#101017)

Building Leadership Capacity in Schools by Linda Lambert (#198058)

Building Shared Responsibility for Student Learning by Anne Conzemius and Jan O'Neill (#101039)

Finding Your Leadership Style: A Guide for Educators by Jeffrey Glanz (#102115)

Leadership for Learning: How to Help Teachers Succeed by Carl D. Glickman (#101031)

On Becoming a School Leader: A Person-Centered Challenge by Arthur W. Combs, Ann B. Miser, and Kathryn S. Whitaker (#199024)

Staying Centered: Curriculum Leadership in a Turbulent Era by Steven J. Gross (#198008)

Audiotapes

Creating New Traditions in Educational Leadership by Leo Corriveau and Raymond McNulty (#200129)

Leadership for the Classroom by Richard Ruffalo (#202255)

The Power and Promise of Meaningful Leadership by Cile Chavez (#299132)

Staying the Course: Building a Vision of Leadership Capacity for Learning by Anne Conzemius and Jan O'Neill (#201152)

Multimedia (Action Tools)

Analytic Processes for School Leaders by Cynthia T. Richetti and Benjamin B. Tregoe (#701016)

Guide for Instructional Leaders: Guide 1 by Roland Barth, Bobb Darnell, Laura Lipton, and Bruce Wellman (#702110)

Guide for Instructional Leaders: Guide 2 by Grant Wiggins, John L. Brown, and Ken O'Connor (#703105)

PD Online Courses

Effective Leadership by Frank Betts (#PD98OC)